FLUCTUATING BORDERS

Speculations about Memory and Emergence

FLUCTUATING BORDERS
Speculations about Memory and Emergence

Edited by Rosalea Monacella and SueAnne Ware

RMIT University Press, Melbourne

Published by RMIT University Press, an imprint of
RMIT Publishing
PO Box 12058, A'Beckett Street,
Melbourne, Victoria 8006
Australia
Telephone 61 3 9925 8100
Fax 61 3 9925 8134
Email: info@rmitpublishing.com.au
http://www.rmitpublishing.com.au

Publications Editor
Brenda Marshall

Production Editor
Noè Harsel

Production
Tim Schork, Michelle Phillips-Schork

Research
Steve Biddulph,Tim Castillo,Lawrence A Herzog, Michael Kearney,
Troy Lovata, Rosalea Monacella, José Parral, SueAnne Ware

National Library of Australia
Cataloguing-in-Publication entry

Fluctuating borders : speculations about memory and emergence
ISBN 9781921166488

1. Territory, National - Psychological aspects. 2.
Nationalism - Psychological aspects. 3. Cultural geography.
4. United States - Boundaries - Mexico. 5. Mexico -
Boundaries United States. 6. Australia - Boundaries. I.
Monacella, Rosalea. II. Ware, SueAnne. III. Royal
Melbourne Institute of Technology.

304.2

Printed in China through Publishing Solutions

INTRODUCTION

01. BORDERS

02. MEMORY

03. TEMPORALITY

04. EMERGENCE

INTRODUC
TION

Fluctuating Borders is a publication which re-considers the possibilities for international borders. In this volume designers and theorists from multiple but cognate disciplines such as Planning, Architecture, Landscape Architecture, Urban Design and the Visual Arts have reflected on and critiqued notions of memory, fluctuation and emergence. This publication begins with examining how Mexico, America and Australia are conceptualised not just in terms of how border spaces are remembered but how they are represented and organised. These countries share a common thread – a colonial past. Australia and America are a part of the Western world, and are regarded as developed nations. Mexico, on the other hand, is positioned on the fringes of the Western world and is commonly understood as a developing nation. Our investigation, here, aims at interrogating and confusing, theoretically and practically, the polarised structure and rigidity of these territorial and national representations by forming connections along lines of difference thus discovering how the outside can be implicated in the inside. Extending the complexity involved in border conditions to other parts of the world, we have also included one example from Israel as expressive of another voice in conundrum. We acknowledge that the material presented in this publication is only a beginning, but nonetheless felt compelled to publish it now to contribute to this on-going dialogue about the possibilities of international borders.

In this introductory chapter we will begin to address these complex border conditions through a series of design speculation projects involving design students from America, Mexico and Australia. In November 2003, students representing five universities from these three countries came together to form a workshop, Border Crossings, which considered the possibilities of international borders rather than their limitations. This chapter offers critical reflections and design propositions from this workshop that can serve as a theoretical framework for the remainder of this book. Specifically, through describing and reflecting upon the design ideas raised in the workshop, this chapter offers a framework that reflects and critiques notions of memory, fluctuation, permeability and emergence. We propose that that the nature of border itself through certain design speculations and interventions can become formless and dynamic, not unlike the indeterminate nature of landscape itself. Border spaces are in a continual state of 'becoming'. We also discuss how design ideas, much like the complex border conditions, are not linear but can intertwine and blur to form other ways of understanding and other sets of readings. It is this intention to provoke readers into reconsidering the intent and values of borders that will be carried throughout the following chapters.

01. PERMEABILITY

The existing physical border crossing at Tijuana and San Ysidro is essentially a barrier structure. On the Mexican side crossing over via car is reminiscent of toll gates where no one has the correct change. There is always a long, slow line, and someone's car is always being turned inside-out while officials search for contraband. The pedestrian crossing is just as conspicuous; long delays and detailed scrutiny into one's purpose for travelling into America are invasive, lengthy procedures. The American side into Mexico rivals a supermarket express lane or a McDonald's drive through. Mexico welcomes you while the US repels you.

It is the space of the Tijuana-San Ysidro border that Border Crossings attempts to act. What was a limiting space governed by tight boundary rules and regulations can become liminal, opening up to other possibilities. For instance, the students installed a series of lighting strategies which celebrate the quantity of cars exiting and entering into Mexico. The gateway, when intervened by this installation, became literally a fiesta of moving lights instead of immutable architectural structures. Another project proposed morphing the border gate itself into a series of ramps and complicated pathways which wind into journeys along the border and do not just serve as routes to either nation's territory. With these ramps and pathways folding upon themselves the gateway space becomes a destination, a labyrinth of experience rather than a barrier into or out of a country. This shifts the emphasis away from who gets included or excluded to one concerned with an occupation of the borderland itself. This design proposition reconsiders slippages and shifts to create another experience of border crossing.

The rusty steel wall demarcates the playa de tijuana from Tijuana

Increasingly connections beyond the constraints of the city's territory have been forged in Tijuana. These new global connections have at times bruised the city's expressive capacity, tying up everyday life within a system of supply and demand. In terms of the border city's futurity, the question that often needs to be explored is how can design activity open the city up to new organisations? Specifically, how can the dynamic history of Mexican culture and the fatal consequences of the border be embraced as an enabling capacity that does not predetermine the form of social, political and cultural life of the borderland, but presents itself as a time of becoming and bifurcation? To do so, one must take into account the border city's diverse modes of exchange including ones that may elude the rationalised and categorised forms of social, political and economical exchanges.

Fencing once used in the cold war is reused to construct the triple fence between Mexico and USA

Categorised social, political and economical exchanges have not only transformed individual and collective human activity but have also permeated the notion of a fixed territory. As such, the city and its border become a kind of product, up for sale, and closed off to their own reinvention. The city considered as another product

The expanse of land which divides Mexico and USA

that enters and service the global market suggests the city as somehow intact and, by implication, inactive. But, the city and its border are only ever partial objects. A territory, as Gilles Deleuze and Félix Guattari suggest, can be considered to be open to its own deterritorialisation. Here we consider a passage from Deleuze and Guattari on the deterritorialisation process:

1   Gilles Deleuze and Felix Guattari, *A Thousand Plateaus: Capitalism and Schizophrenia* (trans: B Massumi), Minneapolis, MN: University of Minnesota Press, 1987, 269.

> Consistency is neither totalizing nor structuring; rather it is deterritorialising... The security, tranquillity, and homeostatic equilibrium of the strata are thus never completely guaranteed: to regain a plane of consistency that inserts itself into the most diverse systems of stratification and jumps from one to the other, it suffices to prolong the lines of flight working the strata, to connect the dots, to conjugate the processes of deterritorialisation.[1]

The city and its border, following Deleuze and Guattari's formulation, are ultimately permeable.

02.RESONANCE

Memory is forged not simply as mere recollection of definite and unproblematised pasts. In the act of remembering that fragment of past which is remembered necessarily becomes something else. The past is forged by the movement of the present. As the philosopher Henri Bergson explicates:

2   Henri Bergson, *Matter and Memory* (trans: NM Paul and WS Palmer), New York: Zone Books, 1991, 168-169.

> Memory, laden with the whole of the past, responds to the appeal of the present state by two simultaneous movements, one of translation, by which it moves in its entirety to meet experience, thus contracting more or less, though without dividing, with a view to action; and the other rotation upon itself, by which it turns toward the situation of the moment, presenting to it that side of itself which may proves to be most useful.[2]

3   ibid, 169.

Memory prolongs the desires of the past into the present. In remembering we may desire something that can never be. Yet, in evoking and desiring the past, memory enables a kind of becoming, a reproduction of the past which is in fact not a mere replication. Bergson suggests that in the act of remembering what is remembered becomes 'an unlimited number of different 'systematizations'.[3] This performative nature of memory, in having the power to question and transform the particularities of *remembered* cities, thus offers a mode which challenges the conventional notion of cities and borders as fixed.

I) The Richness of the Border

The borderland becomes richer with each act of remembering and each recording of a memory. As an expatriate American who spent much of her childhood and, later on, young adulthood, travelling over the border, I cannot help but feel a bit of disgrace when I think about Operation Gatekeeper.[4] In my mind the border has always been an excuse for racism, discrimination and humiliation. Frequent trips across the border caused my mother to be under constant suspicion. Can you imagine the border patrol's reaction to a carload of kids with a single mother crossing up to five times a year to visit our grandmother in Guadalajara and her sister, *mi preferida abuelita*, in Nogales? My childhood memories of crossing the border are filled with the sites and smells of my *abuelita's* village. Nogales was dusty and dry, and exquisitely unsanitary. In the 1970s Nogales was a rough, gritty town with no frills. Yet it was alive, full of vibrant public places, and very much a borderland.

Armed with those memories, I anticipated that Tijuana would also fit within my somewhat romanticised view of border towns. While I was not disappointed, I was unprepared for the intensity of the experience. Sandra Cisneros best describes the transition into Mexican borderlands in her book *Caramelo*:

> As soon as we cross the bridge everything switches to another language. Toc, says the light switch in this country, at home it says click. Honk, say the cars at home, here they say tan-tan-tan. The scrip-scrape-scrip of high heels across the Saltillo floor tiles. The Angry lion growl of the corrugated curtains when the shopkeepers roll them open each morning and the lazy lion roar at night when they pull them shut. The pic, pic, pic of somebody's faraway hammer. Church bells over and over, all day, even when it's not o'clock. Rosters. The hollow echo of a dog barking. Bells from skinny horses pulling tourists in a carriage, clip-clop on cobblestones and big chunks of horse caquita tumbling out of them like shredded wheat.
>
> Sweets sweeter, colours brighter, the bitter more bitter. A cage of parrots all the rainbow colors of Lulu's sodas. Pushing a window out to open instead of pulling it up. A cold slash of door latch in your hand instead of the dull sound doorknob. Tin sugar spoon and how surprised the hand feels because it's so light. Birthday cakes walking out of a bakery without a box, just like that, on a wooden plate. And the metal tongs and tray when you by Mexican sweet bread, help yourself. Cornflakes served with hot milk! A balloon painted with wavy pink stripes wearing a paper hat. Churches the color of flan. Vendors selling slices of jicama with chilli, lime juice, and salt. Balloon vendors. The vendor of flags. The corn-on-the-cob vendor. The pork rind vendor. The fried banana vendor. The pancake vendor. The vendor of strawberries in cream. The vendor of rainbow pirulis, of apple bars, or tejocotes bathed in caramel.[5]

4   It is estimated that over one million people per year cross illegally into the United States from Canada and Mexico mainly for the purpose of employment. Meanwhile, in the daily lives of Tijuanans, 'the *Migra* is playing hide-and-seek with the *mojados* in the hills, kids from an adjacent *colonia* organize a soccer game on the U.S. side. Street vendors sell *tamales*. Artists build illegal installations. And Tijuana simply yawns in the face of its paranoid neighbor across the wall.' (Mike Davis, *City of Quartz: Excavating the Future of Los Angeles*.) The causes and consequences of Operation Gatekeeper will be further discussed in the chapter 'Borders, Memory and the Slippage In-Between'.

5   Sandra Cisneros, *Caramelo*, New York: Vintage Contemporaries, 2002, 17-18.

As per Cisneros' writings, memory can become richer with the sounds and rhythms of words. Likewise design speculations, inclusive of drawings, diagrams and written materials, can enrich and transform *what is remembered*.

03. PERFORMATIVE

It is in this active reconstitution of memories through speculative design processes and projects that new and different understanding of the borderland can emerge. We will explore this theme of emergence through four design projects – *Tijuana, a Designer's Paradiso; Projecto Mohado; La Zebra* and *Symbiocity* – conducted by the students.

November, 2003
Design workshop held at IBERO Americano with students from RMIT, Puebla, UNAM, New School and San Diego Architecture School, Guadalayara

I. Tijuana, a Designer's Paradisio

Mexican public space is in a constant state of appropriation and reconsideration. In Tijuana, market stalls line the public sidewalks along the border crossing. Where the footpath widens there are more merchandise and formal market areas; and where it narrows it is relegated to the small time vendors selling things from their pockets. The photograph-yourself-on-a-zebra stands, unique to Tijuana, have prime locations on street corners with taxi-cabs and bar pimps. Downtown Tijuana is flooded with pharmacies, souvenir shops and *cantinas*. Almost everywhere in the *tourista* zone, you are incredibly aware of your role as consumer, a consumer of Mexican culture and illicit things which you escape from America to do here. What can we as designers learn and utilise from this place? How do these forces, forms, and fallacies offer us a way of acting or speculating?

However, the other parts of Tijuana, where its residents live, offer another way of engaging in the city's fabric. The established neighbourhoods are suburban scaled and interestingly walk-able, yet they ignore the covenants and controls relegated to the pseudo-American type new developments to the city's north. They start as squats; grow, transform and appropriate space as their residents' resources accumulate. The houses here have expectation built into them. Most rooflines have rebar poking through in anticipation of another floor; if they have a concrete slab it is usually partially exposed waiting for a new wing. These houses start as a collection of recycled materials, the *bricolage*, and then evolve, over time, into what we see today. It is easy to romanticise this process; yet it is born out of necessity, culture and practice. The constant state of flux is entirely evident in a place like Tijuana. But, how can designers utilise these forces and practices beyond analytical frameworks and metaphors? This may mean searching for innovative possibilities for the border and the introduction of new forms of markets and territorial situations so that Tijuana does not exist as just a spatial but fixed phenomenon but is also a dynamic temporal phenomenon. To acknowledge the border is not necessarily a support for its function to segregate and hence the implicit conservative-nationalist politics. Rather, to acknowledge it, with depth, is to affirm the transformational processes taking place within the borderland that transgresses the city's physical dimensions. The dimension of time is what facilitates this transgression.

It is this focus on the border as a fluctuating and temporal entity that served as a catalyst for the series of projects developed from the Border Crossing workshop. Particularly the projects attempts to tie time together with the themes of memory and emergence, and thus identify complexities and new possibilities for the city's political and territorial edges. The workshop became an investigation on how an edge can become a transforming un-demarcated event, a temporal being. We now turn to three student projects produced in the Border Crossing workshop that demonstrate the emergence of new possibilities and considerations of borderland spatiality.

II. Projecto Mohado

Projecto Mohado is a series of proposed platforms that are sited in a part of the ocean that intersects the border dividing the US and Mexico. Currently, the physical border, *la linea*, extends far out into the sea in case Mexicans who are interested in crossing the border illegally wish to swim to the US. The fence literally makes those who try to cross swim into a very strong current and become swept out to sea. The shores on both sides are littered with clothing and personal items as a constant reminder of Operation Gatekeeper.

In the students' proposal for *Projecto Mohado* the ideas of memory and border city intertwine and weave together in formal physical outcomes. The project attempts to create a new kind of public space which relies on re-thinking the nature and boundary of international waters. The platforms evoke notions of Mexican plazas or *zocalos*[6] that are fertilised with a layering of multiple programs. The idea of how Mexicans appropriate public space for commerce and the way in which it is always bustling with people becomes sited with a series of platforms isolated in no man's land. The proposed design offers up sites of appropriation rather than rigidly programmed territories. The platforms are connected to Tijuana through a series of pier structures and board walks. The Mexicans have direct access to the platforms whereas the Americans must take a boat. Paradoxically, the borderlands become freely and easily accessible to Mexicans whereas Americans must now make a constrained effort to enter into the border zone.

Inserted into the proposed platform's assemblage of layered surfaces is a memory wall. The wall is a recording device for those who die crossing the border as well as a recording device for the tidal flux and shifts in ocean currents. The wall is a recording device for shadowing and ramping down into the subterranean space. The wall is literally about memory and recording. And, because memories and recordings are always reinscribed, the wall becomes itself a marker in flux. It is a work which is constantly shifting as the quantity of people who encounter it varies.

6 *Zocalos* are traditional Mexican public squares or plaza spaces, and are prominent in most Mexican cities.

In general government or privately appointed designers and planners create an architectural and/or spatial framework which limits the dynamic forces of certain places so that shopping malls can be built for the purpose of commerce. This is in effect is a form of colonisation. However, *Projecto Mohado* does not invest in this form of limiting site appropriation. The series of platforms in the ocean performs another form of site appropriation that challenges the limiting site appropriations found in the borderland's growing commercialisation. This project's strength lies in how it doubles site appropriation practices common to the borderland's public spaces and shopping areas by making site appropriation its own mode of operation and programmatic response to the area's increasingly commercialisation. The memory wall on the platforms is in a state of constant re-appropriation; and this in many ways celebrates the dynamism underlying the seemingly commercialised borderlands.

III. La Zebra

This student design proposition seeks to literally create a new fabric as a way of ameliorating the border and its power. Through erasure, the designers tried to create a new zone of recreation and open space. The diagrams, drawings, models and sketches began as iconic literal translations and abstraction from Tijuana's unique collection of icons, for instance, *La Mujera Blanca*, the painted donkeys, and *La Linea's* arches. This project assumes *tabula rasa* and positions itself in the realm of defining a new kind of fabric and form of the city. It allows Tijuana a fresh start in that it disregards the forces that currently exist and propositions the border as a place to generate a new way of building both the social and the urban fabric.

While this may seem naïve and in some instances insensitive, the detailed study begins to work through a set of criteria for the production of the new. The project takes as its inspiration and *genus loci* that nothing is precious. However, this does not suggest that nothing is significant, rather it suggest that what is treated as precious changes especially given the throw-away economy of America that has infected the borderland's mode of production and conception. *La Zebra* adopts this throw-away economy's mode of operation – newness, reinvention and a reconsideration of the existing – in order to challenge what is made precious in this throw-away economy itself. The bondage to history as absolute is challenged, and thus this project's conceptual framework may be said to be distinctly modernist.

Following this *tabula rasa* mode of operation the project proposes that the existing material and architectural fabric can be cleared to allow a series of triggers such as squatting and soil creeping to take place, as a way of introducing non-telic programs which form can change dynamically depending on frequency of use and climatic conditions. In this sense the project proposes that things like drainage and erosion are forces that enable the rethinking of topographic form and unplanned occupation as a way of generating new programs. The final design work is a suggestion of what could occur given current growth patterns, water catchments, and specific micro-climates but it is open-ended and allows for an anticipated flux.

IV. Symbiocity

The student project *Symbiocity* was an exploration of the border at a much broader scale. The students in this group specifically examined multiple border cities and proposed urban and regional scaled interventions which attempted to benefit both sides of the border. They defined the border as an intense zone of exchange where the people, the economy and the environment are interconnected. To intensify this exchange, they proposed interventions where the residents of Mexico and America could mingle, trade and share in a mutually beneficial way. For instance, in the Tijuana region, they proposed a strategically placed North American international airport, a new sewage treatment plant, a hydro-electric scheme, and a repositioned transport infrastructure to be shared by both San Diego and Tijuana counties. This shared infrastructure allowed for a reconceptualisation of what constitutes the dynamic landscape of the borderland itself.

The politics of such an endeavour would be an essential catalyst for both sides to rethink their mutual reliance, and thus reinvent what makes up borderland communities. The edges of communities become more permeable, for instance the proposed North American airport would neither belong to America nor Mexico but to North America. In doing so a new kind of political, cultural and economical identity that liberates itself from the tyranny of binary divisions between the two nation states is forged. In addition, North America becomes inclusive instead of consisting of just Anglo, English-speaking inhabitants.

CONCLUSIONS ABOUT STUDENT WORK

Tijuana is in a constant state of flux. The aforementioned student projects seek innovative possibilities for the border and new forms of economical and territorial situations, so that the city is not just a spatial phenomenon but becomes a temporal one as well. More specifically, Border Crossings sought to celebrate and register physically crossing the border as a temporal and spatial event. Whereas *Projecto Mohado* and *La Zebra* examined new architectural forms and spatial types as a way of tapping into existing phenomena, *Symbiocity* speculates through shared infrastructures and defined political programs as a means for producing a renegotiated meaning for borders. The projects also attempt to conceptualise fluctuation through ideas of memory and emergence; *Mohado* in a direct literal manner via the memory wall and platforms, and Symbiocity in terms of its transformational processes. However, neither project restricts itself to the city's spatial organisation, but speculates on what a border can offer us in terms of an alternative vision – alternative memories and emergences.

These projects transform our understanding of a place's memorialisation and the institutionalisation by stressing the transitive process and tapping into chaotic forces present in Tijuana's current complexity and dynamicity. In this sense, the acts of memorialisation and institutionalisation can extend beyond the city's governed territorial and political boundaries. Tijuana in this sense becomes more than a generalised impoverished city; instead it offers to us a new understanding of border conditions, a degree of hope and of a different kind of future.

PROVOCATIONS FOR THE PUBLICATION

More often than not an organisation is conceived in terms of its *order*. However, this book aims to reposition what order may be; this means *order* will be reconceived in terms of possible divergences within memory and emergence. Throughout the subsequent chapters we will attend to four main themes – borders, memory, temporality and emergence – in order to reposition what order can be. Some chapters will focus solely on one of the themes while others may combine two or more themes.

I. BORDERS

The first section of this publication will centre specifically on case studies which explore notions of borders and border cities. Borders can be solitary and political entities, however they can also be bodies that are sensitive to a greater context and can be transformed by factors such as social, environmental, political and infrastructural complexities. The nature of what a border is thus changes. For example, the border urban condition presents an intriguing challenge for design researchers. No border zone in the world has experienced the magnitude of urban growth found in the region between the US and Mexico. Indeed, world history suggests that until the late twentieth century, major cities are always located away from international borders. Globalisation has altered the conditions of economic development, enabling many complex transnational processes to occur at the US-Mexico border. These processes include global manufacturing (*maquilas*), immigration, transnational smuggling, and cross-border environmental problems. Taken together these processes make the US-Mexico border region a laboratory for the study of twenty-first-century globalisation and its impact on nation-states and regions. For instance, Lawrence Herzog's chapter on border ecologies, Tim Castillo and Troy Lovata's chapter on border fluidity, and Michael Kearney's chapter on Israel's security wall all speculate on the transformative powers of border urbanism's socio-political forces, albeit from three diverse standpoints.

II. MEMORY

Other chapters investigate and reveal the evolving nature of memory within the urban fabric by considering how the borderland cities themselves can propose new possibilities of urban material organisations, which, in turn, can accumulate and differentiate according to site specificity. The ambition is to produce a diverse range of 'anti-memorials' dispersed and inherent in an evolving urban fabric. For example, Steve Biddulpah's chapter on the Siev X Memorial in Australia and SueAnne Ware's chapter on anti-memorials in Juarez/El Paso begin to position the role of anti-memorials and memory with 'illegal' migration. As Ware elaborates in her chapter, memory is always affected by a complex spectrum of states and stimuli including forgetting, denial, repression and trauma. What is remembered, what can be included to become a memory of a place can thus work against what is considered the place's official past. In fact, both papers are directed toward providing memories that fall outside of mainstream imagination of national boundaries and nationhood.

III. TEMPORALITY

We proposed that *in* time the border itself can become a formless dynamic and complex condition. The indeterminately changing-in-time landscape becomes a useful conceptual tool to think about borders instead of the conventional model of order. Two chapters suggest a shift from an ordered and rigid fabric to a set of systems that operate and emerge from its existing context, thus allowing access to a new form of urban border. Jose Parral's chapter on urban fluctuations considers time and landscape conditions as integral to border cities and concepts also relating to self-organisation. Additionally in this chapter Parral considers how one's self-identity can be transformed in time. The theme of temporality can also be traced in Ware's chapter on memories of borderlands. As she suggests, memories, too, are transformed by the passing of time.

IV. EMERGENCE

The 'urban' understood to be like nature itself, fluctuating, organising and supporting an extensive range of permanent and temporal activities offers to us new modes of organisation. These new modes of organisation can cut across scaled binaries, undoing the binary between the micro and the macro as well as reconsidering the division between the landscape and the built environment or the 'urban'. All in all there are moments in each of the following chapters that will speculate on the formation of these new organisations and systems which express the urban's immanent mode of becoming. Most prominently Rosalea Monacella's concluding chapter frames emergence and self-organisation as new ways of engaging in design research.

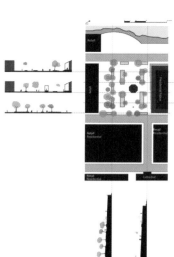

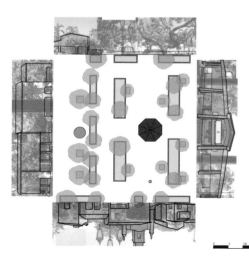

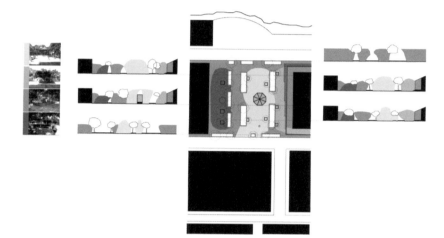

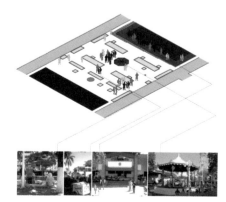

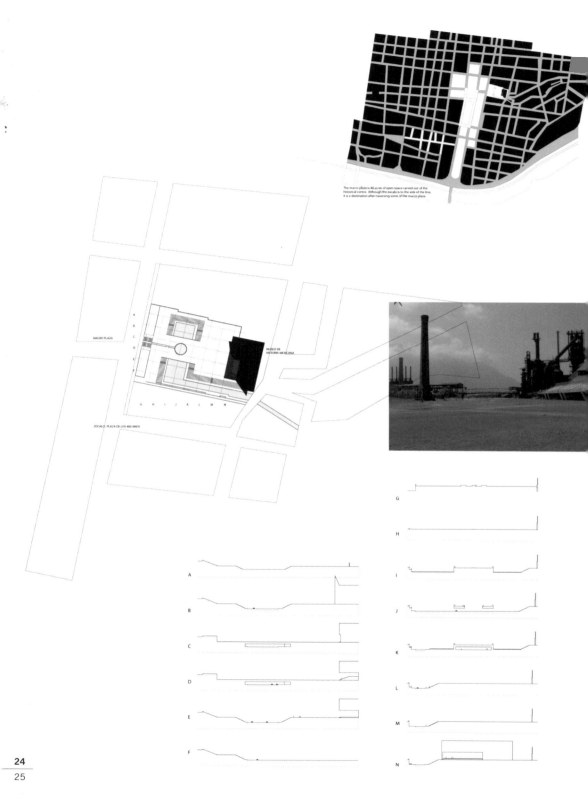

The macro plaza is 40 acres of open space carved out of the historical centre. Although the zocalo is to the side of the line, it is a destination after traversing some of the macro-plaza.

MACRO PLAZA

MUSEO DE HISTORIA MEXICANA

ZOCALO: PLAZA DE LOS 400 ANOS

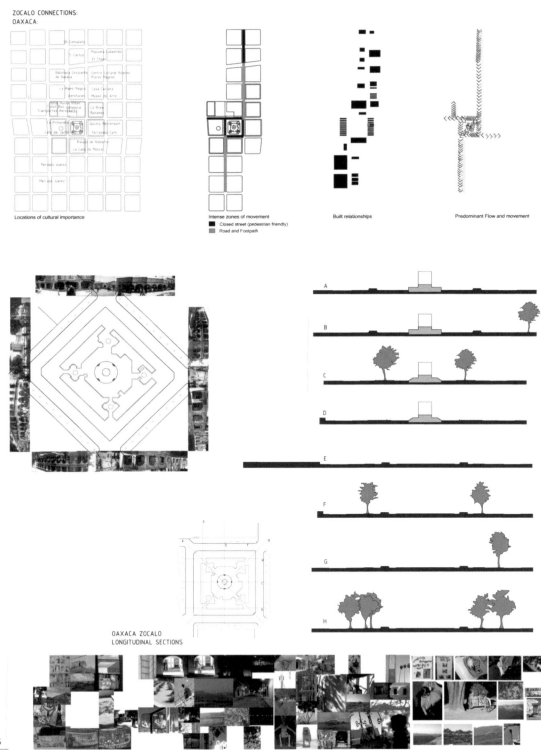

ZOCALO CONNECTIONS:
OAXACA:

Locations of cultural importance

Intense zones of movement
- Closed street (pedestrian friendly)
- Road and Footpath

Built relationships

Predominant Flow and movement

OAXACA ZOCALO
LONGITUDINAL SECTIONS

A
B
C
D
E
F
G
H

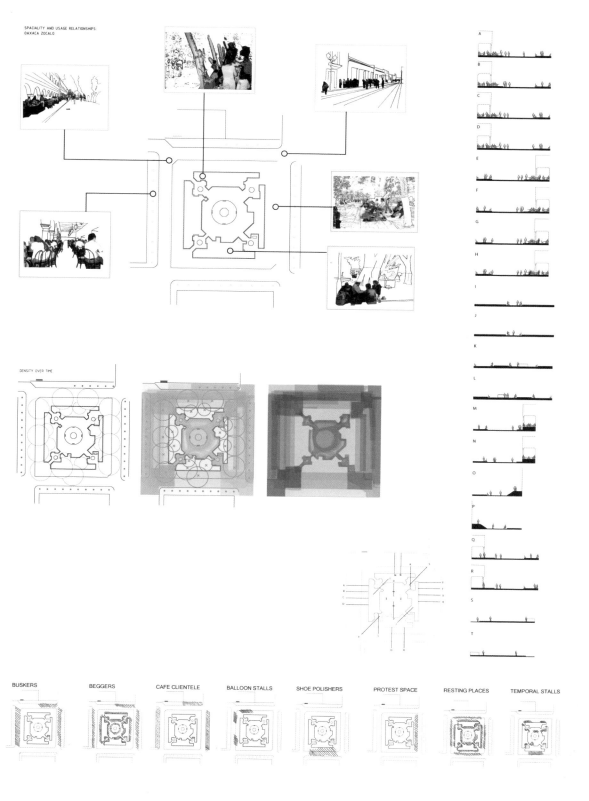

SPACIALITY AND USAGE RELATIONSHIPS
OAXACA ZOCALO

DENSITY OVER TIME

A
B
C
D
E
F
G
H
I
J
K
L
M
N
O
P
Q
R
S
T

BUSKERS   BEGGERS   CAFE CLIENTELE   BALLOON STALLS   SHOE POLISHERS   PROTEST SPACE   RESTING PLACES   TEMPORAL STALLS

01.
BOR
DE
RS

RETHINKING THE DESIGN OF MEXICAN BORDER CITIES: SEVEN ECOLOGIES[1]

Lawrence A Herzog

In the first decade of the twenty-first century, the Mexican border has become one of the Western hemisphere's most important repositories for booming cities and vast global industrial complexes. It is one of the most dynamic economic corridors in the Americas. Its cities are truly hybrid in their form, weaving and borrowing design elements from the interior of Mexico, or from the economic giant just north of the boundary. The border zone is one of the great laboratories of globalisation, and its cities represent a canvas of the work in progress that is transnational urbanism – landscapes that are driven by the triple engines of global assembly, free trade and the international division of labour.

In the growing discourse of 'globalisation' the Mexico-US border has frequently been misunderstood. The importance of its cities has been largely underestimated or even ignored by so called 'global scholars'.[2] The term 'global city' tends to be largely associated with either places that house the headquarters of multi-national corporations (New York, London, Tokyo, etc) or with mega-centres of the third world (Sao Paulo, Shanghai, Mexico City).[3] International border regions have generally been dismissed as marginal places. At the Mexican border, observers imagine 'global' intertwined with drug smuggling, illegal immigration, or violence. But the global ecology of the twenty-first-century border must move beyond these outdated stereotypes. Indeed, border ecologies are now becoming more central to our understanding of global cities.[4] The Tijuana/California border zone offers an excellent laboratory for rethinking the ways globalisation is shaping a new form of urban space.

The 'new borderland urbanism' springs from a simple idea: social, economic, and spatial processes that define urban form are no longer geographically restricted within the boundaries of the nation-state. Globalization means that a set of exogenous forces (foreign investors, transnational workers, etc) are now brought to bear on the local and regional construction of urban form. We can now ask: what happens when those forces, and the ecologies they create, operate within a physical space that overlaps international boundaries? Along the Mexican border, we observe the way urbanism begins to transcend the physical limits of nation-states. Border cities are tangible living spaces that cross national political boundaries. In effect, global processes are being translated into real geographic space. We can call this new global prototype a 'transfrontier metropolis'.[5]

Tijuana, Mexico, offers perhaps the most illustrative example of the new ecology of Mexican border cities. It is a metropolis pulled between the forces of globalisation and those of traditional Mexico. Tijuana is a Mexican city, born to a culture whose urbanism is anchored in the indigenous cosmologies of sacred space and nature as

1 Some of the ideas in this essay are based on a previous work: Lawrence Herzog, 'Global Tijuana', in Michael Dear and Gustavo Leclerc (eds), *Post Border City*, New York: Routledge, 2003.

2 Exceptions to this trend include: Leslie Sklair's *Assembling for Development*, Boston: Unwin Hyman, 1989; and Lawrence Herzog's *From Aztec to High Tech*, Baltimore: Johns Hopkins University Press, 1999.

3 See for example John Short and Yeong-Hyun Kim, *Globalization and the City*, NY: Longman, 1999; Saskia Sassen, *The Global City*, Princeton: Princeton University Press, 1991.

4 See Dear and Leclerc, *Post Border City*, 2003.

5 This concept is developed in two of my prior books: Lawrence A Herzog, *From Aztec to High Tech: Architecture and Landscape Across the Mexico-United States Border*, Baltimore: Johns Hopkins University Press, 1999, and Lawrence A Herzog, *Where North Meets South: Cities, Space and Politics On the U.S.-Mexico Border*, Austin: University of Texas Press/CMAS, 1990.

well as Spanish grid designs of colonial royal power and urban Catholic order. These foundations have been modified by Latin modernity, fused with twentieth-century nationalism, and managed under a highly centralised political system where the federal government dictates the form and function of its cities.

Yet Tijuana's ecology is also being mediated by many new global and transcultural forces; the city is a conduit and homeland to international migrants, a staging area for the new global factory, and the site for experiments in expanded free trade and cross border consumerism. Taken together these divergent forces have generated a metropolis literally caught between paradigms – modernity and post-modernity, north and south, local and global – a place on the verge of being catapulted beyond, to a new level of innovation, or what has been termed hybridity.[6]

6   See for example discussions of hybridity in Gustavo Leclerc, Raul Villa and Michael J Dear, *Urban Latino Cultures Los Angeles*, London: Sage, 1999; and also in Michael Dear, *The Post-modern Urban Condition*, Oxford: Blackwell, 2001, 166-175.

With this in mind, this chapter begins to unravel the landscape of Tijuana's emerging global ecologies. Seven new ecologies form the superstructure of this bustling metropolis of nearly two million people. They include spaces formed by global economic actors (global factory zones, transnational consumer spaces, and global tourism districts) and spaces that represent regional and local responses to globalising forces (post-NAFTA neighbourhoods, transnational community places, spaces of conflict and invented connections).

Global Factory Zones
The 'global factory' is one of the great inventions of late twentieth-century world capitalism. As labour costs impinged on profits among multi-national firms in the 1950s and 1960s, the idea of global cheap labour enclaves emerged. Firms discovered they could simply move the factory floor to a less developed nation. Third World countries suddenly loomed as the new industrial labour pools for global industrial giants. Thus was born the global factory.

Mexico quickly became a key player, through the so called 'twin plant' or *maquiladora* (assembly plant) project. In the 1960s, Mexico's government hatched a new federal office to promote border economic expansion – it was known as PRONAF, the National Frontier Program. The biggest plank in the PRONAF development strategy was reduction of unemployment through industrial growth. In 1965, the Border Industrial Program (BIP) was introduced. The BIP forever changed the Mexican borderlands. In 1970, there were 160 maquiladoras in Mexico, employing around 20,000 workers. Some twenty-five years later, there were an estimated 2400 assembly plants in Mexico, employing nearly three-quarter of a million workers, with a value-added estimated at roughly three billion dollars. All of these plants are foreign owned; the majority come from the US, Japan, South Korea, Canada and Germany.

The factories themselves descend upon the landscape of Tijuana, consolidating around an ecology of the modern industrial park, not unlike the counterpart US suburban industrial parks to the north. As in the US, the dominant feature is the use of uniform lot sizes and street setbacks, as well as controlled landscaping. There are also sophisticated systems of screening and security, as well as large scale parking facilities. The *Ciudad Industrial* (Industrial City) on the eastern Mesa de Otay, is Tijuana's principal global factory zone. Because this *maquila* zone lies on the outskirts of Tijuana, it resembles a kind of suburban hacienda compound,[7] an insular space where workers provide labour to the *'patron'* (the industrial giant) in return for a modest salary. However unlike industrial parks in San Diego, Tijuana's *maquila* parks are surrounded by poor *colonias*, low-income settlements that typically house many of the assembly workers.

7 This idea is discussed in Daniel Arreola and James Curtis, *The Mexican Border Cities*, Tucson: University of Arizona Press, 1993.

Transnational Consumer Spaces

One of the guiding principles of global capitalism has been the 'culture- ideology of consumerism'. Global corporations use advertising and transnational media not merely to sell their products across the globe, but to promote a style of consumption that becomes part of a standardised global culture.[8] Examples of consumption that has been globalised include soft drinks (Coca Cola, etc) and fast food. Part of the success in marketing these commodities globally can be traced to corporate strategies to homogenise consumer tastes. By constructing globally uniform consumer behaviour (through advertising and construction of recognisable images) multinational corporations can better control the marketing of their products.

8 Leslie Sklair, *Sociology of the Global System*, Baltimore: Johns Hopkins University Press, 1991.

This global homogenisation of consumer taste arguably exists not only in food products, clothing or automobiles, but in the built environment as well. The design of shopping malls, fast food restaurants, hotels, resorts, and other urban spaces has become globalised. There are no longer vast differences between shopping mall designs in China, Ireland, Peru or Mexico. Malls have a standardised site plan and design concept – that includes the use of anchor stores, public areas for walking and sitting, food courts, movie theatres, and restaurants. Further, there is a growing trend in renting space to global chain stores that sell clothing, electronics, and other consumer goods in shopping malls around the world. Hotels and resorts often use standardised designs as well. Indeed, many corporate hotel chains believe that travelers like the predictable, familiar designs of hotel chains in the United States and Western Europe, and thus seek to replicate those designs in other cultural settings. Their marketing departments will tell you that consumers prefer the familiar images of their hotel, over the less familiar components of local cultures.

These designs are not merely limited to buildings. The new public spaces of the twenty-first century will be privatised streets, festival marketplaces or giant mall complexes. Increasingly, these consumer spaces seek to replace the traditional downtown as the primary pedestrian-scale gathering place for post-modern city dwellers.

Mexico has embraced the commodified landscape in the NAFTA era. Four decades ago, nationalist and proud Mexico rejected most US commercial enterprises within its borders – there were virtually no McDonald's or Burger Kings, and no US clothing enterprises anywhere in Mexico as late as the 1980s. But since the signing of NAFTA, Mexico has opened its doors to U.S. and foreign business. Today, hundreds of US chain stores and hotels have swept across the Mexican landscape – from Blockbuster Video, Office Depot, and Sears to Direct TV, Costco, and Walmart. Most of the global hotel chains – including Hilton, Hyatt and Sheraton – have also exploded onto the Mexican scene.

Along the international border, the dominance of the US culture-ideology of consumerism has been particularly intense. In the early 1990s, the invasion of fast food outlets in border cities like Tijuana occurred virtually overnight. In the span of one or two years, every major food outlet – McDonald's, Carl's Jr., Burger King, Domino's Pizza, etc – burst onto the urban landscape. Around the same time, small, medium and large shopping centres began appearing along commercial boulevards and highways. In Tijuana, these mini-malls served to interrupt the pedestrian scale of the downtown, since buildings were set back from the sidewalk, while parking lots stood in front. US-style mega-shopping malls also sprouted along the border – Tijuana has two regional -sized shopping malls. US and foreign corporate interests have little trouble selling consumption to Tijuana and other border city residents. Most Mexican border city dwellers can use satellite television to receive programming from southern California. An enormous, captive Mexican audience can therefore be reached by advertisers on California channels. Mexican consumers learn how to consume, partly by watching American television. As a result, Mexicans living along the border have proven to be highly motivated customers on the US side. Studies in California have shown, for example, that Mexican consumers have similar, if not better information and a slightly better understanding than California residents of locations and qualities of stores and products in the San Diego region.[9]

9 See Lawrence Herzog, *From Aztec to High Tech*.

Global Tourism Districts

Tourism development adheres strongly to the principles of the culture-ideology of consumerism. A central premise of tourism design is the manipulation of visitors' experience of place to maximise profit. Global tourism investors and corporate decision makers tend to view regions as stage sets for generating profit, rather than as genuine places whose identity should be protected. Because global developers generally view investments from distant world headquarter cities like New York, Chicago, or San Francisco, they often lose touch with the places their investments are transforming. The main strategy of tourism development is to enhance marketability and client interest through the production of landscapes that satisfy the needs of projected users.[10] Studies have shown that tourists prefer comfort, reliability and pleasure, especially in foreign settings. The architecture designed to accommodate visitors, which one writer calls the 'tourism gaze', is, in effect, a landscape socially constructed for a targeted population. It has been compared to Foucault's 'medical gaze', a strategy of controlled design aimed at a different economic interest group – consumers of medical services and facilities.[11]

10 ibid.

11 John Urry, *The Tourist Gaze*, London: Sage, 1990.

Tourism developers seek to create homogenous, readily distinguished, easily consumed built environment experiences for their client populations. Controlled resort structures with recognisable designs (oceanfront boardwalks, small, clustered, shopping and restaurant complexes, hotels, fast food outlets, global boutiques) have become the central pillars of tourism landscape design. The value of tourist space is measured by its marketability for short-term tourism visits, rather than by its cultural uniqueness or environmental purity.

The distinct marketing strategies of the international tourism industry lead to the production of placeless landscapes, devoid or destructive of culture and nature. If tourism is more profitable in built landscapes that are homogenous, then what incentive can there be for tourism developers to preserve the original landscapes of the places they invest in? Even in ecologically sensitive zones (jungles, mountains, etc) or culturally preserved spaces (colonial downtowns), the demand for cosmopolitan infrastructure by tourists – luxury hotels, swimming pools, and plush shopping spaces – has the effect of diminishing the original cultural landscapes, which become overwhelmed by structures designed for consumption.

In Tijuana, the main commercial street in the old downtown tourism district, Revolution Avenue, is a striking example of a manipulated, commodified space. Revolution Avenue is to Tijuana what Main Street, USA is to Disneyland – an artificial promenade that sets

MEXITLAN, the Mexican version of Disneyland

12 JB Jackson, 'Other directed houses,' in Ervin Zube (ed), *Landscapes: The Selected Writings of J.B. Jackson*, Amherst: University of Massachusetts Press, 1970.

the mood for a carefully choreographed experience. In Disneyland, the visitor parks his/her car, and walks across the parking lot, through the entrance gates, and onto Main Street, a theatrical stage set, built at 4/5 scale, and lined with costumed characters, from Mickey Mouse to a Barbershop Quartet. In Tijuana, tourists park their cars in vast lots just north of the border, cross the pedestrian entrance into Mexico, and move along a path that leads them into Revolution Avenue.

Revolution Avenue is a mini theme park – a clever stage set of outrageous colour and grotesque facades. Buildings resemble zebras or Moorish castles. Flags and colourful blimps fly overhead. Music blares, whistles blow, barkers shout along its nearly one mile length. The setting is a classic 'other directed space', a vacation-land and consumer haven created for outsiders.[12]

One could argue that Revolution Avenue was designed to be an idealised 'Mexico-Disneyland', a fantasy exotica of what Americans imagine Mexico to be. Ironically, Tijuana entrepreneurs tried to build a Mexican version of Disneyland called Mexitlan, a theme park that celebrated Mexico's architectural history. By the late 1990s, the border theme park was a ghost town that had gone out of business. Its demise points to an apparent marketing error made by Mexitlan designers. Along the border, American tourists prefer a landscape of the exotic and the fantastic. For them, the border's magnetism lies in the world of the unknown, the imagined. Mexitlan gave tourists beautifully designed glimpses into Mexico's real architectural history. This kind of serious tourism experience works in central Mexico but not along the border.

Tourism breeds 'enclavism', the creation of isolated zones for visitors, buffered from the everyday city, to allow the outsider's fantasy of the place to remain distinct from its reality, which is usually less exotic. Enclavism leads to the creation of artificial tourism districts that become segregated from the city itself. In Tijuana, globalised enclaves include Revolution Avenue, the aforementioned Mexitlan, commercial/entertainment complexes in the River Zone, and beachfront tourism zones.

Post-NAFTA Neighbourhoods

The traditional social geography of Mexican border towns reveals an inverse model of the US pattern. In Mexico, wealthy residents cluster in older established neighbourhoods adjacent to downtown, or along a commercial corridor leading out of the central business district. Middle class, working class, and poor neighbourhoods are arrayed concentrically around the core, with the poorest residents living farthest from the centre.

Globalisation exacerbates this social geography; at the same time, it adds new twists to it. The biggest changes are the addition of new residential enclaves for transnational investors and visitors. In Tijuana, the valuable coastline just beyond the city offers comparatively inexpensive real estate for US residents, either in the form of second homes, or permanent dwellings for retirees. Some 25,000 Americans reside in the coastal corridor between Tijuana and Ensenada, and that number will grow.[13] Global real estate projects are aiming to create golf resorts, beachfront condo complexes and luxury marina housing enclaves for foreign residents. These high paying land users routinely outbid Mexicans for coastal properties; the result is that the social ecology of the coastal strip is global – it is dominated by foreign residents.

Meanwhile, US-style condominiums and suburban housing developments for Mexicans have accelerated across Tijuana. Mexican consumers are familiar with US housing, both from crossing the border, or through the print and visual media. Global advertising has altered their taste in housing. Wealthy consumers want condominiums with jacuzzis, sunken bathtubs and satellite television. Even poor migrants aspire to US house-types.

As mentioned earlier, worker housing has been dispersed around the *maquila* zones. Migrants to Tijuana live on the edges of the city, near or beyond the zone of *maquila* workers, in squatter communities of sub-standard housing, also known locally as *colonias populares*. This class of marginal, disenfranchised urban poor may not ultimately benefit greatly from globalisation, but they respond to its seductive pull. The struggle of the urban poor to survive in booming, globalising cities constitutes a key debate underlying the globalisation protest movements around the globe.

Colonias are pockets of haphazardly constructed houses, built by the poor themselves, usually on the worst possible sites in the city – flood-prone canyons, steep sloping hillsides, airports, major highways, or land far removed from the city proper. Many of these settlements were created by illegal land invasions, since the poor do not have liquid capital to pay the cost of a home purchase or even rent. This means that *colonia* residents live in a precarious state burdened by the dual limitations of inadequate house materials for construction (cardboard, tar paper, scrap wood, scrap metal) and questionable legal ownership. Further, these *colonias* often lack basic services like running water, sewage disposal, paved roads, or street lighting. Most of the households use pirated electricity, stolen from illegal lines connected to nearby electricity grids. As NAFTA's grip strengthens along the border, more global economic activities – factories, commercial developments, tourism enterprises – create a higher demand for low paying jobs. This in turn attracts even more migrants from the interior of Mexico. Globalisation has exacerbated an already burgeoning migration stream headed north, thus spreading the landscape of squalid shanties across the hills and canyons on the outskirts of Tijuana. In the midst of increasing wealth in certain privileged areas (coastline, downtown, river zone), there is increasing deprivation scattered through the squatter communities in the region.

13 Mexican property law does not allow foreigners to own land; however post-NAFTA legislation makes it possible for foreigners to lease land through a trust or *fideicomiso* arrangement for up to sixty years.

Transnational Community Places

The development of a transnational urban ecology is an overlooked dimension of globalisation. A century ago, territorial politics dictated that nations meticulously guard their international boundaries. This shelter function mentality[14] fostered a common pattern of national settlement: the largest concentrations of urban population tended to locate away from the physical edge of the nation state. In fact, before 1950, boundary regions were mainly viewed as buffer zones that served to defend the larger nation from land-based invasions. Under these conditions, few significant community spaces evolved on or near national boundaries. Indeed important urban settlements did not appear near borders.

Yet today, globalisation is opening up border territories to new community formations. Citizens on either side of the Mexico-US boundary are increasingly drawn together; old differences are set aside as urban neighbours become part of a common transnational living and working space. The building blocks of these new transnational communities lie in the social and physical linkages that connect settlements across the boundary. Such linkages in Tijuana-San Diego include the existence of international commuters, transnational consumers, global factories, cross-border land and housing markets and transnational architecture.

14 The notion of 'shelter function' is defined in Jean Gottman, *The Significance of Territory*, Charlottesville: University of Virginia Press, 1973.

The evolution of a community of transnational citizens that have a presence north and south of the border is expressed in the social ecology of the region. Urban dwellers do not merely consume goods, they consume the built environment itself – by purchasing land and housing on both sides of the line. NAFTA has opened the door for purchase or lease of land by global investors along the border, particularly in the Baja California region, where plans for international resorts, hotel complexes, commercial development and luxury housing are abundant. Baja California already has the second largest enclave of expatriate American homeowners (the largest lies in the Guadalajara region), with some 15,000-20,000 Americans residing in homes along the Baja coast. Meanwhile, increasing numbers of Mexican immigrants, as they legitimise their work and immigration status, are purchasing homes on the US side of the border. Some members of a family may live on the US side, while others remain on the Mexican side.

One of the more vivid examples of transborder community place-making is visible in the strategies employed by border residents in taking back the boundary zone itself. The wall, legally managed by the State, is being physically re-incorporated into the adjacent communities by users, be they local residents, border crossers, artists, or community political groups. Rather than let the boundary zone continue to be a space of liability, a no-man's land, a zone of insecurity, potential crime and international bureaucracy, local citizens are choosing to humanise the border. Monuments to people who died crossing the boundary have been erected on the border fence itself. The fence is transformed into a public space that can be visited by local residents, a sacred place that commemorates the regional struggle at certain moments in history.

This grassroots place-making seeks to redefine the boundary space, turning a negative (smuggling, illegal immigration, border police forces) into a positive (works of art, monuments and commemoratives that are part of the community). People who live near the fence use it to define their living space – gardens are planted, clothesline may connect to it, telephones are installed for use by the clandestine border crossers. The boundary zone becomes not only a part of the everyday neighbourhood landscape, it is textured into the built landscape of migration, redesigned as a conduit to help those Mexicans who are desperate to cross the frontier and work in the United States. Why not let them make the phone calls to their families north of the border?

Spaces of Conflict
For more than a century, Mexican border cities like Tijuana were defined by their connection to the physical boundary. They existed in a schizophrenic dance between the reality of economic ties to the United States versus nationalist links to Mexico. The physical boundary – the wall, the fence – stood as a constant reminder of this double identity.

Today, globalisation along the border evokes a critical debate – does the region's future lie with perpetuation of the wall, and all that it symbolises – national security, sovereignty, defense, and militarisation – or does it reside in the propagation of a world of transparent boundaries and trans-frontier cities? This theme shapes an underlying tension embedded in the built environment of border cities, a tension that is manifest by the conflicted landscapes of the immediate boundary zone where the two nations meet.

The globally familiar icon of militarised boundaries is the Berlin wall – an image that brings to mind barbed wire, concrete barriers, soldiers in watch towers peering through binoculars, and bodies of failed border-crossers draped across the no man's land between East and West. The German wall, before its destruction, ran sixty-six miles in twelve-foot high concrete block, thirty-five miles in wire and mesh fencing. It had over 200 watchtowers, and blinding yellow night lights mounted on tall poles.

The Tijuana-San Diego 'wall' is forty-seven miles long, and built from corrugated metal landing mats recycled from the Persian Gulf War. Migrants have punched it full of holes, so a second parallel wall is under construction a few hundred feet north. The new wall includes eighteen-foot high concrete 'bollard' pilings topped with tilted metal mesh screens, and an experimental cantilevered wire mesh style fence being developed by Sandia Labs. The fence/wall runs toward the Pacific Ocean, where it becomes a ziggurat of eight, six and four-foot-high metal tube fence knifing into the sea. It is buttressed by six miles of stadium nightlights, 1200 seismic sensors and numerous infra red sensors used to detect the movement of people after dark.

15   Alan D Bersin, US Attorney, San Diego, cited in Joseph Nevins, 'The law of the land: Local-national dialectic and the making of the United States-Mexico boundary in Southern California', *Historical Geography*, vol 28, 2000: 41-60.

Like the Berlin wall, landscapes along the Tijuana boundary explode with messages of danger and conflict. These images tend to reduce the border to a cliché, a war zone, a place controlled by national governments and their police forces. Signage on fences and along the line reinforces an underlying theme – that only the governments can decide who enters and who crosses. The US government's Operation Gatekeeper, a strategic 1994 plan launched by the US Immigration and Naturalization Services, has been a striking example of a national policy determined to re-'Berlinise' the California-Mexico border. Indeed, one official claimed that the goals of the operation were to 'restore the rule of law to the California-Baja California border'.[15] This general theme of 'militarisation' along the border has remained as part of the landscape, always threatening to move to the forefront each time a crisis looms. The September 11, 2001 terrorist event in the US had the immediate effect of resurrecting the policing, enforcement-oriented functions of the international border.

Invented Connections

The image of the border as a place of violence and chaos has, for many decades, acted as a built-in form of redlining. Border uncertainty and risk depressed the value of land around the line for most investors. As a result, many boundary zones attract only low rent land uses, such as warehouse storage facilities, parking lots, or currency exchange houses. Properties frequently remain vacant or abandoned, while landowners wait to see what governments have planned for the future. This risk traditionally created a vacuum for investors; yet it also opened the window for those willing to gamble that NAFTA might ultimately transform the boundary zone into a place to do business.

The San Ysidro-Tijuana port of entry/border zone is the single largest bi-national connector along the US-Mexico border. Thirty-four million vehicles and over seven million pedestrians cross through this gate each year. But the port of entry and surrounding zone on both sides of the border are fragmented by a variety of land use and design problems – from traffic congestion, poor circulation routes, and disorganised land uses, to crime, public safety concerns, and unresolved land development plans. This vital physical space, the anchor for the region's cross-border economic development, needs to be carefully planned and redeveloped in the next decade.

In a globalising world, the border zone may no longer be able to function purely as a 'pass through' space. It is becoming a connector for the regional economy, and even an important destination in its own right. Thousands of transnational citizens utilise this space each day. Indeed, much of the 'pass through' space could be converted to

16   This point is developed in a new book, Lawrence A Herzog, *Return to the Center: Culture, Public Space and City Building in a Global Era*, Austin: University of Texas Press, 2006, chapter 7, 'The Globalization of Urban Form'.

the kinds of public spaces found in any city – plazas, gardens, promenades.[16] Trade and tourism flourish here. The border town of San Ysidro has a population of some 20,000 inhabitants, about ninety per cent of whom are of Mexican origin. Downtown Tijuana lies a few hundred yards further south of the line, and houses over 100,000 inhabitants within a radius of one mile of the border.

If there is one single characteristic of the Tijuana/San Ysidro crossing zone today it might be termed a crisis of image. This zone is ripe for an 'invented connection', a new ecological space created when global investors or entrepreneurs seek to alter the built environment. Large-scale privately funded development projects at boundary crossings are in various stages of completion along the entire two-thousand-mile boundary. These projects envision a number of different types of developments, mostly mixed use, and medium density. A prominent feature is that they are mainly privatised spaces, with partnerships maintained with relevant public border monitoring agencies.

On the San Diego-Tijuana border, adjacent to the San Ysidro crossing, a private firm purchased large tracts of land, and with the Redevelopment Authority of the City of San Diego government, put together a new, large-scale project called 'Las Americas'.[17] The investment plan for this space imagines a new future for Mexico's boundary – an integration of pedestrian walkways, gardens and plazas with private retail, entertainment, hotel and office buildings. What is novel about this vision is its recognition of the boundary itself as a space of community life, rather than a space of instability, conflict and smuggling. Of course, it also signals the discovery of the potential revenues to be gained by private sector interests in allowing the border to become a privatised place.

17   Land Grant Development, *International Gateway of the Americas*, Project Proposal, San Diego, 1997.

Conclusion: Weaving it all Together

How do the seven ecologies 'knit together' to form a 'transfrontier metropolis'? Seven 'ecologies' have been offered, each one a reflection of the global processes that are redefining the Mexico-US border and the cities that reside along it. Global investors and other actors seek to reshape border cities to suit their specific interests. This, in turn, is producing a new social ecology with changing building strategies and architectures, and new kinds of gathering zones, public spaces, community niches, and business districts.

The design of these new border cities is underscored by the theme of contradiction in the landscape. Examples include the 'war zone' mentality at the line itself versus the transnational idea of free trade. On a micro level, one sees this in the contrast between the chaos at the Tijuana/San Ysidro border gate, and the promise of a new 'Las Americas' cross-border commercial project.

Other unresolved conflicts in the design of border cities lie in emerging pedestrian scale districts in the old downtown versus suburban, car-oriented shopping centres; American-style condo complexes and wealthy suburban enclaves, as against the tar paper shacks and dusty streetscapes of the poor *colonias*. In the end, the global landscape is one of contrast and contradiction – between rich and poor, investment and disinvestment, labour and capital, modernity and post-modernity, planning and spontaneity.

BORDER FLUIDITY: EMERGENCE ON THE AMERICAN/MEXICAN FRONTIER

Tim Castillo and Troy Lovata

Abstract

The cities of El Paso, Texas and Ciudad Juárez, Chihuahua, form an expanding metropolis of over two million people. Although a national border, between the United States of America and the United Mexican States, formed on the Rio Grande River acts to segregate and demarcate the two communities, this area is a contiguous urban sprawl that continues so far as to encompass part of the adjacent American state of New Mexico. It is simultaneously a hard border and a fluid frontier across which people, goods and ideas flow in both directions. This paper maps emergence in this region. It is an interdisciplinary exercise between architecture and archaeology which traces cultural, economic, technological, and media boundary processes.

Complexity and Emergence

The complex reality of living along borders stands in stark contrast to the simplicity of a line on a political map. In the past the co-authors of this paper, one an architect and the other an archaeologist, have found value in interdisciplinary research – including studies of the impact that the performance of culture and the unyielding presence of landscapes have on Southwestern display and touring spaces.[1, 2] We believe that the complexity of border conditions merits a similar cross-disciplinary examination that combines experience with material culture and cultural change with an understanding of form, spatial organisation and visualisation. Archaeology is an especially useful partner in this collaboration because of recent attempts by archaeologists, like Bradley Parker,[3, 4] to generate 'terminology, models or conceptual frameworks that allow cross-disciplinary supra-regional comparisons of frontier dynamics'.

We, the co-authors, have spent substantial portions of our lives in fair proximity to different sections of the 1952 miles (3141 kilometres) border between the United States of America and the United Mexican States. Both of us currently live and work in Albuquerque, New Mexico – which lies a few hundred miles in from the international political boundary and the fast-growing, cross-border metropolis of El Paso, Texas/Ciudad Juárez, Chihuahua.[5] We don't live on the border, but we do see ourselves as part of a wider region that is both shaped by and broaches this international boundary. We are cognizant of the economic differences between the northern and southern halves of this region, but we are also aware of the cultural links that pre-date the contemporary border and political structure. After all, New Mexico and Texas were once part of Mexico and all were part of the Spanish empire prior to Mexican independence. We generally agree with Timothy Brown,[6] who finds that this is a unique region because, 'to most Mexicans, their northern states, with half their nation's land but only one-fifth its people, seem too American, a bit alien, vaguely un-Mexican,' and likewise, 'to many Americans, their own Southwest sometimes

1   Tim Castillo and Troy Lovata, 'Action makes place', in Ron Rael (ed), *South:* vol 1, South Carolina: Clemson University, 2005.
2   Troy Lovata, 'Flattening the sky: Experiencing the intersection of landscape and technology on the plains of St. Augustin', in Tim Castillo (ed), *Design for the Very Large Array*, Albuquerque: College of Architecture and Planning, University of New Mexico, 2004.

3   Bradley J. Parker, 'Toward an understanding of borderland processes', *American Antiquity*, 71(1):77-100, 2006, 77.
4   Bradley J Parker and Lars Rodseth, *Untaming the Frontier in Anthropology, Archaeology and History*, Tucson: University of Arizona Press, 2005.

5   INEGI. *XII Censo General de Poblacion y Vivienda 2000*, Distrito Federal, Mexico: Insituto Nacional de Estadistica, Geografia e Informatica, 2001.

6   Timothy C Brown, 'The fourth member of NAFTA: The U.S.-Mexico border', *Annals of the American Academy of Political and Social Science*, 550:105-121, 1997, 109-110.

7   Brown 1997, 110.

8   George W Bush, 'Remarks following a tour of the border in Yuma, Arizona, May 18, 2006', *Public Papers of the Presidents*, Washington DC, 22 May 2006.

9   Timothy J Dunn, *The Militarization of the U.S-Mexico Border, 1978-1992: Low-Intensity Conflict Doctrine Comes Home*, Austin: University of Texas Press, 1996.

10   Alan D Bersin, 'El Tecer Pais: Re-inventing the U.S./Mexico Border', *Stanford Law Review*, 48(5):1413-1420. 1996.

11   Parker 2006.

12   ibid, 91.

13   City of El Paso, *Southbound Border Crossings: From El Paso to Juárez, Totals by Bridge: 2004*, City of El Paso Street Department, Texas. http://www.ci.el-paso.tx.us/planning/_documents/bridges_data-2004.pdf, viewed September 2004.

14   US Customs Service, *Northbound Border Crossings: From Juárez to El Paso, Totals by Bridge: 2004*, US Customs Service, Office of Public Affairs, El Paso, Texas. http://www.elpasotexas.gov/planning/_documents/International%20Bridge%20Traffic%202004.pdf, viewed April 2005.

15   Bridge-crossing data is skewed northward in part because, unlike the US Customs Service, the City of El Paso has not included the Bridge of the Americas or the Santa Teresa Port of Entry (which lies just outside city limits) in their southbound totals. But the sheer volume is apparent nonetheless.

seems similarly alien and terribly Hispanic'. However, this idea that, 'the U.S.-Mexican border is unique for what it unites, not for what it divides…'[7] is contrary to repeated attempts over the last three decades – rising to the fore again just this year[8] – by the US federal government to militarise the border, erect impenetrable fences, and define people on the north and south sides of this region as culturally separate.[9, 10] The goal of this paper is to begin to explore this contrast.

Bradley Parker has developed an interdisciplinary model for systematically understanding borderland processes which serves as the framework for this paper.[11] Parker defines an overarching concept of a borderland that is made up of a continuum between borders which are static and restrictive, and frontiers which are porous and fluid. He stipulates that categories, also known as boundary sets, refine this model. These include: geographic sets (which encompass topography, climate, flora and fauna, and natural resources); political sets (entailing the administrative and military); demographic sets (with sub-categories of ethnicity, population density, health and gender); cultural sets (from the linguistic to religion to material culture); and economic sets (relating to the extraction, trans-shipment, and production of commodities and finished goods). These sets are dynamic units and the interactions between them characterise a boundary at specific times and in specific places. In short, boundary sets define something as a borderland. However, not all boundary sets are necessarily operating in similar fashions and they can even run counter to each other. Emergence is a key concept in this system because, 'each of the boundary sets has the potential to influence any other boundary set', and, 'as we move through time the relationships between the various types of boundaries represented in the model vary'.[12] Parker's model allows researchers to describe how boundaries function and how they developed, but it also forces the realisation that neither conditions nor explanations are locked.

The Movement of People: The El Paso-Los Angeles Limousine Company
The idea of moving, whether legally or illegally, between the United States and Mexico is often focused on the act of the crossing the political border itself. The massive number of people traveling over the El Paso/Juárez bridges emphasises this act and marks this area as a crucial point for cross-border traffic. For instance, in May 2004 – a month by no means out of the ordinary – the City of El Paso's Street Department counted over 250,000 private passenger vehicles and 23,000 pedestrians heading southbound.[13] In the same month the US Customs Service clocked over 1.3 million private passenger vehicles and 700,000 pedestrians crossing northbound.[14, 15]

But the El Paso/Juárez metropolis is not just a major border crossing at an isolated point on the landscape. Rather, it is a key node in an extensive regional travel network that links the American Southwest and Mexican north. The border's congestion, document checks and extensive security are contrasted by people using the area's bridges as a midpoint in travel deep from, and deep into, the region's interior.

The huge number of people traversing El Paso/Juárez bridges cross in many different ways – from foot to private vehicle to a number of separate bus systems. Intra-regional bus service plays an integral role in both crossing the border and defining the metropolis as a node for travel further afar. There are a number of bus companies that are licensed and insured on both sides of the border and cater to a focused, regional clientele.[16] They, unlike American nationwide services such as Greyhound, are often advertised in bilingual or Spanish-language ads and only in locations with large immigrant populations. They are often cheaper than Greyhound for point to point travel between large cities and smaller towns with large Hispanic populations. The El Paso-Los Angeles Limousine Express company operates one of the largest of such bus systems. The company began as an on-demand car service providing limousines for individual travel between El Paso and Los Angeles, but it no longer has any limousines in its fleet. The company changed over entirely to scheduled-service buses to better accommodate an expanding number of Mexican riders and changes in the ways that they travel. Today it uses El Paso/Juárez as the central node in a north/south/west route system. It now also serves Phoenix, Arizona, and Las Vegas, Nevada, to the west and runs between Ciudad Chihuahua and Cuauhtémoc, Chihuahua and Albuquerque, New Mexico, and Denver and Greeley, Colorado, on a north to south axis.

Consumption: Examples of Economic and Cultural Boundary Sets

Emerging, and re-emerging, Hispanic populations are having measurable impacts on commerce in the American Southwest. The products they purchase, the services offered to them and the ways in which these are marketed reflect changing demographics. For example, journalists have noted that population shifts are driving changes in the items sold in, physical layout of, and popularity of grocery stores in Greeley, Colorado, an agricultural and food processing hub that has attracted ever larger numbers of Hispanic workers.[17] A survey of the El Paso-Los Angeles Limousine Express's route shows similar shifts occurring across the region.

First, an array of Mexican and Mexican-inspired products is available at grocery and convenience stores in the towns of Anthony, Hatch, and Truth or Consequences, New Mexico. Some of these stores cater to travelers as they move along the bus route up from El Paso/Juárez; while others serve populations that reside or work at the buses' final destinations. They offer, alongside traditional American and New Mexican consumer goods: horchata and agua fresca from the same type of dispensers used for Coca-Cola and Pepsi fountain drinks; foodstuffs made in Mexico; products from multi-national, Hispanic companies like Gamesa (packaged on both sides of the border); international money wiring services such as Western Union; and even advertisements for cross-border bus companies. New Mexico is historically linked to Mexico, but the territory has long been noted for having a singular character that sets it apart from other areas in the cross-border region.[18] Historians often point to the state's relative isolation prior to the twentieth century and the early dates of Spanish settlement along the northern Rio Grande to explain New Mexico's uniqueness.[19] It is not surprising to find some regionally shared consumer goods, but there are noticeable differences

16   Whatcom Council of Governments. *IMTC Cross-Border Transit Study, White Paper #3: Survey of Existing Cross-Border Transit Services*, Whatcom Council of Governments, International Mobility & Trade Corridor Project, Whatcom County, Washington.

17   Anonymous. Neighborhood Store. *Greeley Tribune (Colorado)*. http://www.greeleytrib.com/apps/pbcs.dll/article?AID=/20010708/WORLDSAPART/112310258, viewed 8 July 2001.

18   Jorge Iber and Arnoldo De León, *Hispanics in the American West*, Santa Barbara: ABC-CLIO, 2006, 65.

19   Iber and De León, 2006, 65-66.

between the contemporary concepts of New Mexican and Mexican – even though the concept of Hispanic has a role in both – in New Mexico. The goods and services offered along the El Paso-Los Angeles Limousine Express' route are beginning to blur these differences and the people who purchase those goods are redefining New Mexico as part of a larger regional identity. They indicate a re-emergence of supra-regional, cross-border culture.

Second, the presence of a Camino Real Hotel both in Ciudad Juárez and at a prominent point (between the convention centre and plaza) in downtown El Paso indicates another kind of cross-border emergence/re-emergence. Camino Real hotels and resorts, named after the royal Spanish road that traversed colonial-era Mexico, is a high-end Mexican chain with locations throughout the country. The recently built, 360-room El Paso hotel is their first location outside the country. Its heated pool, health club, business centre, and choice of causal and fine dining cater to a different clientele than the economic migrants which Americans usually associate with cross-border travel. It also represents American recognition and acceptance of a Mexican brand identity since not just Mexicans are lodging within.

Finally, emergence and the solidification of supra-regional culture are evident in the type of consumer experiences offered south of the border as well as corresponding types of architecture – such as fast-food restaurants and big-box retailers built in styles ubiquitous north of the border. Brands and corporations – and their building designs and layouts – associated with and based in the United States are increasingly visible in and around Ciudad Juárez. Our survey notes that Ciudad Juárez is now home to American chain stores such as Wal-mart, Costco, Office Depot, Autozone, True Value Hardware and Home Depot; franchised American restaurants including Applebee's, Denny's, Subway, Kentucky Fried Chicken, Carl's Jr. and Peter Piper Pizza; and American chain hotels such as Holiday Inn Express. Similar to the operation of the Camino Real in El Paso, these establishments are catering not only to Americans traveling in Mexico, but to Mexicans themselves. While some Mexicans are moving north as economic migrants, a growing middle- and upper-class are now being serviced by American companies that once operated only in the US. These populations are now both receiving and demanding the array of goods and services they've experienced to the north.

Cultural and Linguistic Boundary Sets: FM Band Radio

20 Parker 2006, 87.

Archaeologist Bradley Parker[20] notes that language is a key ingredient in group identity and that, 'although notoriously difficult to delineate, when linguistic geography can be worked out it has often added considerable depth to the characterization of borderlands'. Many of the people who reside around El Paso and Juárez have a shared Spanish language base that historically precedes English.[21] Informally, this would appear to link both sides of the Mexican and American border. Yet language, like the movement of people, has an intangibility that is difficult to map because there are major differences in language skills and whether Spanish is a first or second or a home

21 Iber and De León, 2006, 375-76.

BORDER

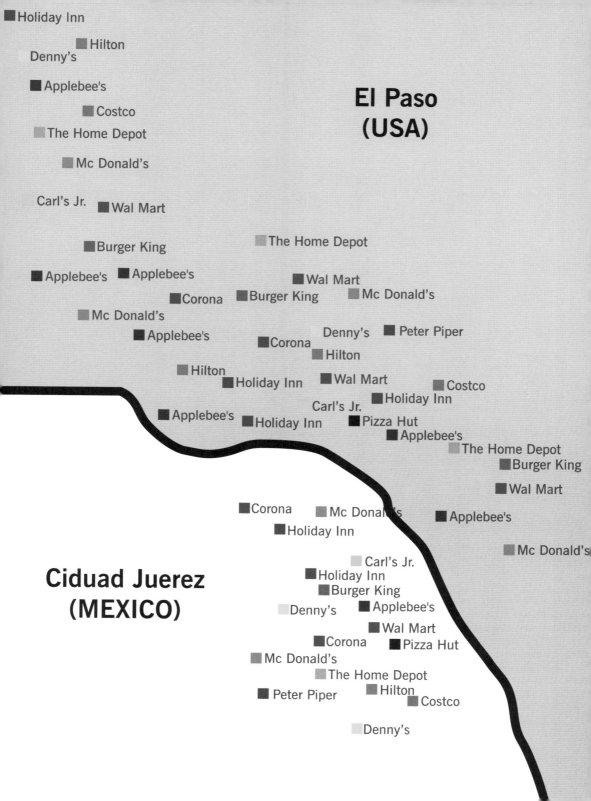

USA

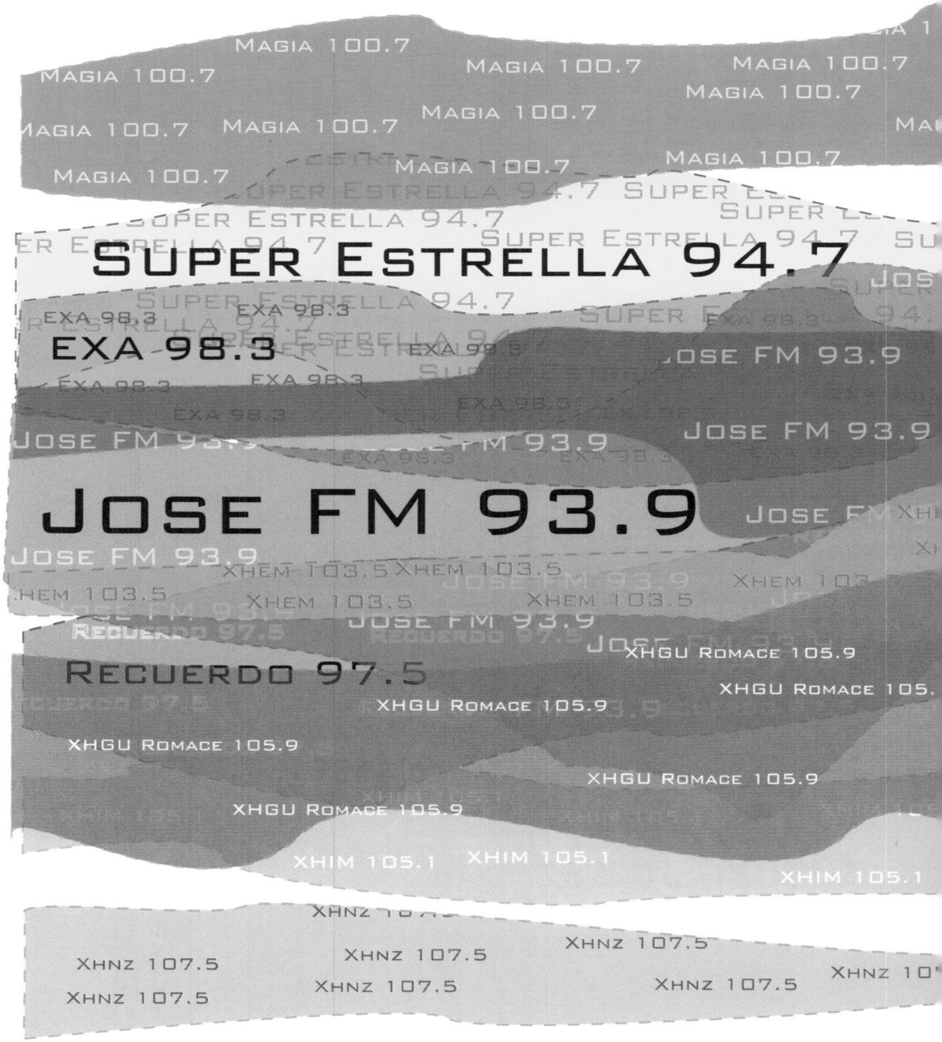
Magia 100.7
Super Estrella 94.7
EXA 98.3
Jose FM 93.9
Xhem 103.5
Recuerdo 97.5
XHGU Romace 105.9
XHIM 105.1
Xhnz 107.5

Mexico

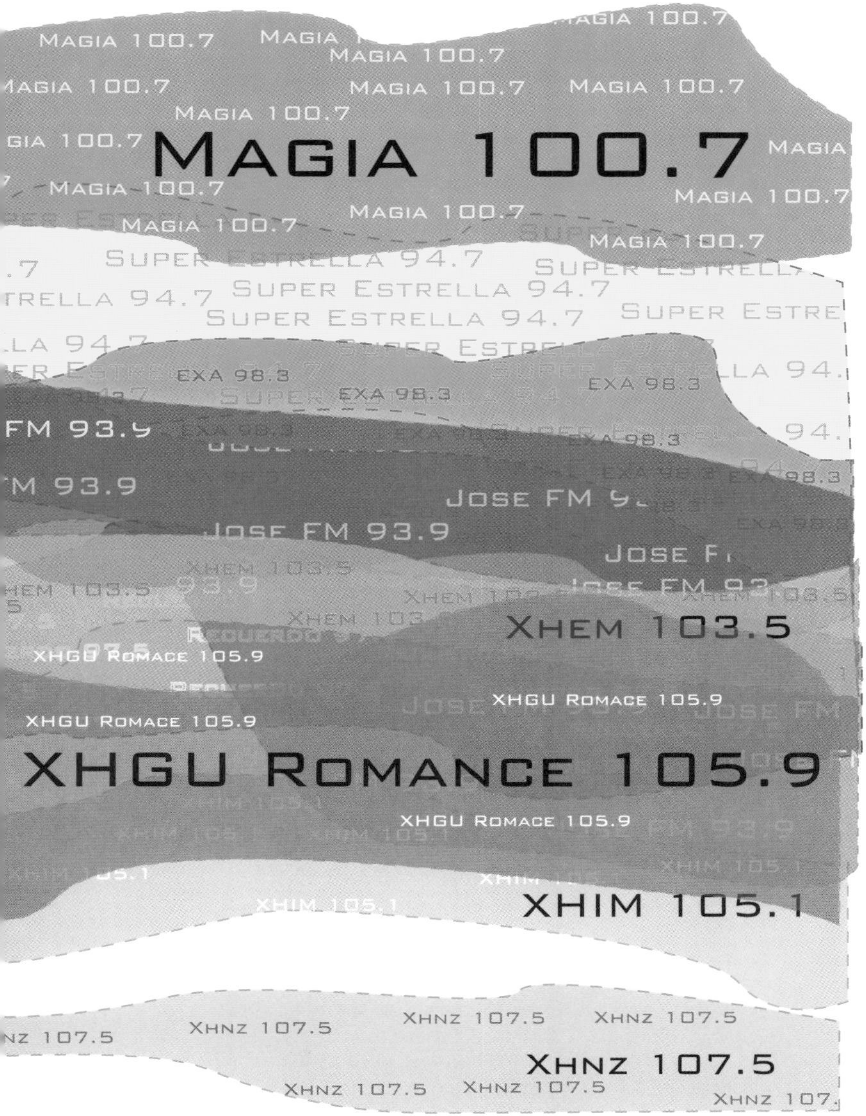
Magia 100.7
Super Estrella 94.7
Exa 98.3
Jose FM 93.9
Xhem 103.5
XHGU Romance 105.9
XHGU Romace 105.9
XHIM 105.1
Xhnz 107.5

or work language.[22] However, the examination of Spanish-language and Spanglish (a Spanish-English patois) radio broadcasts can help delineate cultural affiliation across the El Paso/Juárez metropolis. Lou Orfanella [23] observes that 'radio has the power to individualize its presentation within the mind of each and every listener. There is an intimacy and shared vision that it creates'.

Business reporter Vic Kolenc notes that the El Paso/Juárez Spanish-language and Spanglish radio market is especially vibrant and competitive.[24] There is a wide range of FM stations in the region that broadcast different types of music, talk, news, religious programming, and sports. Recuerdo FM (97.5 MHz) currently broadcasts a Mexican oldies music format. The station is owned by Los Angeles-based media conglomerate Univision and has long been dominant in the ratings. Recently, Recuerdo FM's position has been challenged by increasing listener interest in José FM (93.9 MHz), which broadcasts a variety of old and new music, and Exa-FM (98.3 MHz), which provides contemporary Spanish and Spanglish dance music. José FM is owned by Los Angeles-based Entravision, which operates a similar station in Monterrey, Nuevo Leon (a near-border metropolis to the southeast of El Paso/Juárez), and Exa-FM is owned by MVA Communications of Mexico City. Other popular FM frequency stations include Romance, Super Estrella and Magia.

Lou Orfanella's sense of radio-generated intimacy and unanimity does appear to be at work in El Paso and Ciudad Juárez. Radio towers stand atop the different mountains that overlook the two halves of the metropolis. Broadcasts from each side of the border are clearly received by the other. The same promotional bumper stickers – festooned with radio call letters, frequencies and nicknames – are noticeable on vehicles in both El Paso and Ciudad Juárez. Billboards along the main thoroughfares advertise stations and highlight the competition for drive-time listeners. The range of broadcasts is audible from the rolled down windows of cars crossing the international bridges in both directions. Radio – especially FM broadcasts that transmit a strong, clear, stereo signal – offer a popular soundtrack for intra-regional travel.

Observations

The El Paso/Juárez borderland condition is the product of a dense set of cultural and physical interactions. It is further complicated by the emergence of new social structures built on national foundations, but specific to the boundary region itself. This project was meant to be an experiment in understanding and mapping these factors – a process complex enough to warrant an interdisciplinary perspective. We have identified a key dynamic in the regional border condition: the cross-border movement of people through a central node in a much larger system. This was used to further explore other boundary sets – media, linguistic and commercial – which present a picture of the region as a fluid cultural entity instead of two distinct locales separated by a hard and impermeable political barrier. There are obviously many more boundary sets worth exploring and available for mapping and study. But this experiment has been successful in validating an interdisciplinary approach. Archaeology and architecture

22   ibid, 7-8.

23   Lou Orfanella, 'Radio: The intimate medium', *The English Journal*, 87(1):53-55, 1998, 55.

24   Victor Kolenc, 'Hey, José: El Paso Spanish station flies with unusual format', *El Paso Times*. http://www.elpasotimes.com/business/ci_3847474, viewed 21May 2006.

both depend on identifying and then reacting to – by building either explanations or physical constructions – the material manifestations of culture. The theory of one discipline and the data organisation of the other can be applied in concert to produce a meaningful picture of a complex situation.

THE VIOLENCE OF CONSTRUCTION: INTERNATIONAL LAW AND ISRAEL'S ANNEXATION WALL

Michael Kearney

The Occupation

In the four decades since the 'six-day' war of 1967, Israel's military occupation of the West Bank and Gaza has been consolidated and standardised through a continuous assault on both the people and the physical environment of the occupied Palestinian territories. The Israeli grip on Palestinian territory has been ensured by means of a 'violence of construction'; the establishment and expansion of illegal settlements, combined with a network of Israeli-only bypass roads have created the facts on the ground required to prevent the realisation of Palestinian self-determination in the form of an independent and sovereign state in the West Bank and Gaza.

As demonstrated by the collapse of the Oslo Accords, after negotiations between the Israeli Government and the Palestinian Authority which continued throughout the 1990s, ownership and control of territory underlies the prolonged Israeli occupation. Under the terms of the various agreements concluded as part of the Oslo process, the Palestinian Authority were ceded authority over and responsibility for the Palestinian population in the major urban areas, while Israel retained and gradually increased its control over roads and the movement of people and goods, as well as valuable water resources, airspace and, crucially, most of the land.

Not only did the illegal settlements and the by-pass road system remain intact during the years of negotiations and compromises, but the settler population in the occupied territories increased from over 100,000 to current levels of over 400,000 with expansion continuing unabated. In 1998, Ariel Sharon, then Israel's Minister of Foreign Affairs, outlined the rationale of this policy when he stated that, 'Everybody has to move, run and grab as many hilltops as they can to enlarge the settlements because everything we take now will stay ours…Everything we don't grab will go to them.' The 'them', in this instance is a reference to the Palestinian population whose right to self-determination in the West Bank and Gaza has been repeatedly acknowledged at the United Nations, yet whose dispossession continues daily.

Throughout the decades of occupation, the increase in the settler population came to signify the crushing of the Palestinian nation. Rotbard has identified how in the occupied territories today 'we find two countries superimposed one on the other: on top, 'Judea and Samaria', the land of settlements and military outposts, bypass roads and tunnels; and underneath, 'Palestine', the land of villages and towns, dirt roads and paths.'[1] Since the outbreak of the al-Aqsa Intifada in September 2000, Israel's construction of the Annexation Wall in the West Bank has been intended to make this proximity of separation a permanent reality.

1   Sharon Rotbard, 'Wall and tower (Homa Umigdal): The mold of Israeli architecture', in Rafi Segal and Eyal Weizman (eds), *A Civilian Occupation: The Politics of Israeli Architecture*, Tel Aviv: Babel, 2003.

When construction began in June 2002, world attention remained transfixed by the spiralling death toll resulting from the violence which had followed the Israeli army incursions into Palestinian cities during Operation Defensive Shield. While the violence has remained constant throughout the intervening years, the role of the Annexation Wall in Israel's policy of unilaterally determining borders, and its effect on the welfare of the Palestinian people has come to the fore in commentary and analysis of the prospects of a solution to the conflict.

The Wall's construction is today closely linked with Israel's policy of acting unilaterally to set the borders it wishes with Palestinians. What were once viewed by the wider international community as isolated incidents of land confiscation and the exploitation of Palestinian water and agricultural resources, must now, in the context of such a massive attempt to create new 'borders', be viewed as a central element of the annexation of as much Palestinian territory as possible to Israel, and the ensuing fragmentation of the remainder of Palestine into Bantustans.

The Annexation Wall: Whither the Green Line?
Physically, the Wall is a brutal combination of medieval force and Orwellian control. It is comprised in large part of massive concrete walls complete with watch towers. Such is its appearance in and near Palestinian urban centres. The city of Qalqilya, with a population of 40,000, is completely encircled by an eight-metre-high wall, and the single remaining access road is dominated by an Israeli military base and roadblock. At other points, the structure consists of layers of razor wire, military patrol roads, sand paths to trace footprints, ditches and surveillance cameras which are located either side of a three-metre-high electric fence. A 'buffer zone', from which Palestinians are excluded, and in which houses and other structures have been destroyed, ranges from thirty to 100 metres on each side of the Wall.

More than half of the estimated 700-kilometre route which the Wall is set to follow has already been completed. The first stage of construction began in the north of the West Bank, running south from Jenin to Tulkarm and Qalqilya. Vast stretches of Wall now divide the city of Ramallah from its hinterland and from Jerusalem, stifling movement and commerce, while Palestinian communities within East Jerusalem have been splintered by the Wall.

Israel justifies the construction of the Wall on security grounds, claiming that it will protect Israeli civilians within the Green Line from attack by Palestinian militants. The Green Line is the armistice line from the conflict of 1948-49 which followed from the UN sanctioned partition of Palestine into two states. It is not an international border, but rather is regarded as a temporary frontier, which was long assumed to provide a basis for final status negotiations. Since 1967, and the Israeli occupation of the remainder of historical Palestine, the *de jure* position of the Green Line as the basis for negotiations has been made untenable by the blurring of the distinction between Israel proper and the occupied territories, a process greatly enabled by the settlements and by-pass roads.

With the imposition of the Wall as a 'fact on the ground' Palestinian negotiators are in an extremely weak position should they seek to base negotiations on the Green Line as the frontier between Palestine and Israel. Eighty-five per cent of the Wall is to be built on the West Bank, with only the minimum necessary to avoid Israel having to rapidly incorporate large Palestinian urban centres, such as Qalqilya, actually built along the Green Line. Were the security of Israeli civilians the primary purpose of this Wall it could well have been built entirely along the route of the Green Line, yet not only does it now jut deeply into the West Bank, but is even projected to plough through Palestinian land in the Jordan Valley near Jordan's international border. In such a manner, the Wall will eventually come full circle and completely enclose two significant swathes of Palestinian territory, one to the north of Jerusalem and the other to the south, each divided by a large bloc of central settlements. Furthermore in East Jerusalem and the areas adjacent to the city, which are all part of the West Bank, though labelled the 'Jerusalem Envelope' by Israel, the Wall has already created a third distinctive region that is being effectively annexed to Israel.

One result of this action is the isolation of many thousands of Palestinians between the Green Line and the Wall itself. Cut off from the rest of the West Bank, many villages have been isolated in a Seam Zone which the UNOCHA has estimated will cover 10.1 per cent of the entire West Bank.[2] Moayad Hussin, the mayor of one such village, Baqa al-Sharqia, noted that 'If the fence is for security, if the fence is to keep us out, then why aren't we on the other side? With every kilometre of fence Sharon builds we are sure there is only one answer. This is not about security, it is about land and resources.'[3] Other towns and villages have had the Wall constructed close to the edge of their communities, thus isolating them from their agricultural holdings, olive groves and wells. The effect of this is to ensure that the land in the Seam Zone will lie uncultivated, denying Palestinians their livelihoods and leaving the land open to exploitation.

The effect of the Wall in the area of East Jerusalem is particularly egregious. Once the hub of Palestinian economic, social and cultural activity, Jerusalem has been gradually severed from the rest of the West Bank. This process began with the construction of large settlement blocs, and now by the Wall is to extend eighty kilometres in the Jerusalem area, cutting fourteen kilometres into the east of the West Bank to grasp large settlements close to Israel. Of the 230,000 Palestinians holding East Jerusalem identity cards, three-quarters will be isolated from the West Bank, whilst the remainder will be excluded from Jerusalem. It is clear that whereas the direct result of the Wall is the annexation of Palestinian territory to Israel and the isolation of Palestinians from their neighbours (including Israelis) and the international community, the indirect result is increased pressure on Palestinians to relocate from the Seam Zone and other areas severely affected by the Wall.[4]

The weight on political over security concerns in the choice of the Wall's route through Jerusalem was highlighted when the Israeli minister in charge of Jerusalem admitted

2 UNOCHA, *Preliminary Analysis: The Humanitarian Implications of the February 2005 Projected West Bank Barrier Route*, United Nations Office for the Coordination of Humanitarian Affairs: New York, February 2005, 2.

3 Chris McGreal, 'Caged', *The Guardian*, 3 September 2003.

4 Al-Haq, *Waiting for Justice: Al-Haq: 25 Years Defending Human Rights (1979-2004)*, Ramallah, West Bank: Al-Haq, 2005, 199.

5 Mark Lavie, 'Barrier meant to ensure Jewish majority', *Associated Press*, 11 July 2005.

6 Yuval Yoaz, 'State to court: Fence route has 'political implications'', *Haaretz*, 14 July 2006.

7 International Covenant on Civil and Political Rights (ICCPR), UNGA Res. 2200A (XXI), (1966), 999 UNTS 171, entered into force 23 March 1976.

8 International Covenant on Economic, Social and Cultural Rights (ICESCR), UNGA Res. 2200A (XXI), (1966), 993 UNTS 3, entered into force 3 January 1976.

9 'Concluding observations of the Human Rights Committee: Israel', CCPR/C/79/Add.93, para. 10.

10 'Concluding observations of the Committee on Economic, Social and Cultural Rights: Israel', E/C.12/1/Add.27.

11 'The Fourth Geneva Convention Relative to the Protection of Civilian Persons in Time of War', 12 August 1949, 75 UNTS 287.

12 The Hague Regulations of 1899 and 1907 constituted a significant development in international humanitarian law. In 1946 the International Military Tribunal at Nuremberg stated with regard to the Hague Convention on land warfare of 1907 that, 'The rules of land warfare expressed in the Convention undoubtedly represented an advance over existing International Law at the time of their adoption...but by 1939 these rules ... were recognized by all civilized nations and were regarded as being declaratory of the laws and customs of war' (available at *41*st *American Journal of International Law*, 1947, 248-249). The rules embodied in the regulations were partly reaffirmed and developed by the 'Two Protocols Additional to the Geneva Conventions of 1949' adopted in 1977.

13 'Advisory Opinion on the Legal Consequences of the Construction of a Wall on the Occupied Palestinian Territory', 9 July 2004, General List No. 131, paras. 101, 111-12.

that that the planned route of the Wall in East Jerusalem 'also makes Jerusalem more Jewish'.[5] According to data provided by B'Tselem, an Israeli human rights organisation, of the 430,000 settlers in the West Bank, 380,000 will be brought within the Seam Zone by the route of the Wall. Further evidence that the Wall is intended to provide a 'border' was provided in December 2005, when the then Israeli Justice Minister Tzipi Livni (currently Foreign Minister) announced that the Wall would serve as 'the future border of the State of Israel' and that 'by means of its rulings on the separation fence the [Israeli] High Court was sketching the borders of the state'.[6]

The Annexation Wall under International Law

The international law applicable to Israel's occupation of the West Bank and Gaza includes the main international human rights treaties to which Israel is a party and international humanitarian law (the laws of war). Israel is a party to both the International Covenant on Civil and Political Rights (ICCPR),[7] which is primarily concerned with rights of political participation such as the right to a fair trial, and freedom of expression, and the International Covenant on Economic, Social and Cultural Rights (ICESCR)[8] which is concerned with rights such as the freedom to form trade unions, and the rights to adequate shelter and to food.

Although Israel has consistently argued that it is under no obligation to apply the rights guaranteed in these Covenants to Palestinians in the occupied territories, its interpretation of the applicable law has been roundly rejected by the monitoring Committees for each Covenant. The Human Rights Committee – the ICCPR's monitoring body – has clearly stated that 'the Covenant must be held applicable to the occupied [Palestinian] territories and those areas of southern Lebanon and West Bekaa where Israel exercises effective control'.[9] Similarly, the monitoring Committee of the ICSECR holds the view that Israel's 'obligations under the Covenant apply to all territories and populations under its effective control'.[10]

So long as Israel is occupying territory which is not its own it is also obliged to apply the fourth Geneva Convention Relative to the Protection of Civilian persons in Time of War of 1949.[11] Therein are set forth the rights and duties which Israel has with regard to the population of the West Bank and Gaza. Israel has signed and ratified the Geneva Conventions and is thus legally bound by them, yet it has refused to accept that the Conventions are applicable to the occupied Palestinian territories, arguing that only the older, Hague Regulations only the older, Hague Regulations, are applicable.[12] Academics, NGOs and governments have clearly made the case that Israel is bound by each of these Conventions with respect to its actions in the occupied territories, a view that was confirmed in the Advisory Opinion of the International Court of Justice in July 2004.[13]

The legality of the Wall's construction will be examined under four headings: the confiscation and destruction of property which construction entails; the freedom of movement implications; the principle of non-discrimination; and the prohibition on the acquisition of territory through the use of force.

i) Confiscation and Destruction of Property

Israel has seized control of the land upon which the Wall is being built through the issuing of orders of 'confiscation for military needs'.[14] Although formally these are temporary orders, given the undeniably permanent nature of the Wall, it is likely that they shall be extended indefinitely. Homes and agricultural resources including olive groves, wells and greenhouses in the path of the Wall, in addition to those located in the buffer zone, have already been destroyed by the Israeli Army and many more are scheduled to meet the same fate.[15]

Article 17 of the Universal Declaration of Human Rights provides that 'Everyone has the right to own property alone as well as in association with others' and that 'No one shall be arbitrarily deprived of his property'.[16] Article 17(1) of the ICCPR provides that 'No one shall be subjected to arbitrary or unlawful interference with his privacy, family, home or correspondence...', while Article 11(1) of the ICESCR affirms that 'The States Parties to the present Covenant recognize the right of everyone to an adequate standard of living for himself and his family, including adequate food, clothing and housing, and to the continuous improvement of living conditions...' By confiscating and destroying Palestinian homes in the vicinity of the Wall, Israel is in continuing violation of its obligations under international human rights law as set forth in these legal instruments which together form the International Bill of Rights.

As regards international humanitarian law, Article 52 of the Hague Regulations allows for the requisitioning of property in occupied territories if it is 'for the needs of the occupying army'. The confiscation of the land upon which the Wall is being built fails to satisfy this test since any such confiscation must be an exceptional and strictly necessary measure. Furthermore, the provision requires that requisitions 'shall be in proportion to the resources of the country'. It is explicit at this juncture that the amount of land that is being taken to build the Wall can in no way be regarded as being proportionate to the resources of the Palestinians which are already desperately low. In this instance the Wall is not being built for the 'needs of the occupying army' but rather to serve the broader 'security' policy of the occupying power. Frits Kalshoven, an eminent legal scholar, has stated that since 'the construction of fortifications [serve] (future) military operations of the Occupying Power', they cannot be claimed as being necessary for the needs of the army.[17]

Article 53 of the fourth Geneva Convention prohibits the destruction of real or personal property by an occupying power, unless 'such destruction is rendered absolutely necessary by military operations'. Article 147 of the Fourth Geneva Convention includes among the Grave Braches liable to penal sanction under its Article 146, the 'excessive destruction [...] of property, not justified by military necessity and carried out unlawfully and wantonly'. Such actions may also be considered as a war crime under Article 8 of the Rome Statute of the International Criminal Court.[18]

In order to justify the destruction of civilians' property in occupied territory by reference to military necessity, the occupying power must demonstrate that there is both a

14 'Order Concerning Confiscation of Land Number T/09/02 (Judea and Samaria region)', 2002.

15 'Preliminary Analysis of the Humanitarian Implications of the April 2006 Barrier Projections: Update 5', United Nations Office for the Coordination of Humanitarian Affairs occupied Palestinian territory, July 2006.

16 'Universal Declaration of Human Rights', UNGA res. 217A (III), UN Doc A/810 at 71 (1948).

17 Frits Kalshoven, *Constraints on the Waging of War*, Geneva: International Committee of the Red Cross, 1987, 55-56.

18 'Rome Statute of the International Criminal Court', UN Doc. A/CONF.183/9.

genuine military exigency and that the level of destruction is proportionate with the military advantage gained. Given the prolonged temporal period over which the Wall is being built and the massive amounts of property being destroyed, Israel's destruction of Palestinian agricultural land, homes and other structures along the route of the Wall is in patent violation of both international human rights and humanitarian law since it can neither be regarded as necessary nor proportionate.

ii) Freedom of Movement

The Annexation Wall presents a permanent obstacle to the free movement of Palestinians, whose ability to travel freely within the occupied territories is already restricted by the enforcement of strict and prolonged closures of towns and villages and through the imposition of lengthy curfews. The UN's Consolidated Appeal for the OPT in 2004 emphasised the effect which restrictions on freedom of movement are having: 'Unable to move from villages to cities by vehicle or between cities within the occupied territory without a permit, these obstacles have decimated the Palestinian economy.'[19]

19 OCHA, *Consolidated Appeals Process: Humanitarian Appeal 2004 for Occupied Palestinian Territory*, 18 November 2003, 4.

Article 12(1) of the ICCPR asserts that everyone has the right to freedom of movement within their own state. As Israel is obliged to ensure that the Palestinians under its jurisdiction enjoy the rights set forth in the ICCPR, the restrictions on movement resulting from the construction of the Wall and by the imposition of closures in areas adjacent to it is manifestly illegal and must be reversed.

Commenting on restrictions on freedom of movement imposed in the occupied Palestinian territories, the International Committee of the Red Cross has stated that it views:

> The policy of isolating whole villages for an extended period of time as contrary to International Humanitarian Law (IHL) particularly with respect to those aspects of IHL which protect civilians in times of occupation. Indeed, stringent closures frequently lead to breaches of Article 55 (free passage of medical assistance and foodstuffs), Article 33 (prohibition on collective punishments), Article 50 (children and education), Article 56 (movement of medical transportation and public health facilities and Article 72 (access to lawyers for persons charged) of the Fourth Geneva Convention.

20 International Committee of the Red Cross, 'Israel and occupied/autonomous territories: The ICRC starts its closure relief programme', 26 February 2001.

> While accepting that the State of Israel has legitimate security concerns, the ICRC stresses that measures taken to address these concerns must be in accordance with International Humanitarian Law. Furthermore, these security measures must allow for a quick return to normal civilian life. This, in essence, is the meaning of the fourth Geneva Convention which is applicable to the Occupied Territories.[20]

These statements were made in relation to the policy of localised closures in force in the West Bank. The construction of the Wall will have a far greater negative impact on the lives of the Palestinian population since its immense size and permanency, and the ensuing destruction to property which its construction entails, is likely to render a 'quick return to normal civilian life' an impossibility.

iii) The Principle of Non-Discrimination

An underlying principle of all international human rights law as well as the Geneva Conventions is that of non-discrimination on grounds such as race, colour, sex, language, religion, political or other opinion, national or social origin, property, birth or other status. Nonetheless, each of the violations noted above are being carried out by Israel in a discriminatory manner. Since October 2003 when the Israeli military commander for the West Bank declared the Seam Zone a 'closed area', Palestinians wishing to travel through the Wall to the Seam Zone, including East Jerusalem, cannot do so unless they have been granted permits from the Israeli authorities, a requirement which is not imposed on Israeli citizens or residents (including Israeli settlers in the occupied Palestinian territories), or on non-citizens who are allowed to immigrate to Israel under The Law of Return (1950).[21] Similarly, property destruction and the restriction of movement within, to and from the occupied Palestinian territories is being carried out solely against the Palestinian population, while contemporaneously the movement of more Israelis to new illegal settlements is being facilitated by state incentives and subsidies.

iv) Acquisition of Territory

International law is clear that the occupation of territory must be a temporary matter and that the final status of any territory so occupied can only be determined during negotiations between the relevant parties, in this instance the Israeli and Palestinian people.

The acquisition of territory through the use of force is strictly prohibited under international law. Although conquest was a recognized and important basis for title until the early years of the twentieth century, it is now well established that 'the territory of a state shall not be the object of acquisition by another state resulting from the threat or use of force'.[22] Such action is contrary to Article (2)4 of the United Nations Charter which provides that 'All Members shall refrain in their international relations from the threat or use of force against the territorial integrity or political independence of any State, or in any other manner inconsistent with the Purposes of the United Nations',[23] and the 1970 Declaration on Principles of International Law.[24] The abolition of the legality of acquisition of territory by conquest includes a prohibition on the acquisition of territory through any war including a war of self-defence.[25] Thus, United Nations Security Council Resolution 242, which was passed after the 1967 War, emphasised the 'inadmissibility of the acquisition of territory by war', and called for the 'withdrawal of Israeli armed forces from territories occupied in the recent conflict'.[26]

The prohibition on annexation is reflected in many provisions of international humanitarian law. Though not explicitly prohibited by the Hague Regulations of 1907, annexation of territory through the use of force is clearly incompatible with its spirit and aims. Article 55 precludes the permissibility of annexation by requiring that public and state properties in the occupied area be administered 'in accordance with the rules of usufruct', a situation that can never be reconciled with annexation. Article 47

21 op cit, Al-Haq, 184.

22 DJ Harris, *Cases and Materials on International Law (Fourth Edition)*, London: Sweet & Maxwell, 1991, 201.

23 'Charter of the United Nations, June 26, 1945, 59 Stat. 1031, T.S. 993, 3 Bevans 1153', entered into force 24 Oct 1945.

24 'The Declaration on Principles of International Law concerning Friendly Relations and Cooperation among States in Accordance with the Charter of the United Nations', UNGA res. 2625 (XXV) 24 October 1970, para.10.

25 John McHugo, 'Resolution 242: A legal reappraisal of the right-wing Israeli interpretation of the withdrawal phrase with reference to the conflict between Israel and the Palestinians', *51 International and Comparative Law Quarterly*, 2002, 851.

26 UN Doc. S/RES/242 (1967) 22 November 1967.

27 Jean Pictet, *Commentary: IV Geneva Convention*, Geneva: International Committee of the Red Cross, 1958, 275.

28 ibid.

29 HRC, 'General Comment 12: the Right to Self-determination of Peoples, (Article 1)', March 1984, paragraph 1.

30 See for example: Security Council res. 252 (1968), Security Council res. 465 (1980), General Assembly res. 56/32 (2001). In Security Council res. 478 (1980), the Security Council responded by Israel's adoption of the Basic Law claiming Jerusalem to be the state's capital by asserting that stated that the enactment of that Law constituted a violation of international law and that 'all legislative and administrative measures and actions taken by Israel, the occupying Power, which have altered or purport to alter the character and status of the Holy City of Jerusalem . . . are null and void'. It further decided 'not to recognize the 'basic law' and such other actions by Israel that, as a result of this law, seek to alter the character and status of Jerusalem'.

31 Report of the Special Rapporteur of the Commission on Human Rights, John Dugard, on the situation of human rights in the Palestinian territories occupied by Israel since 1967, submitted in accordance with Commission resolution 1993/2 A, E/CN.4/2004/6, 8 September 2003, 8.

32 'Advisory Opinion on the Legal Consequences of the Construction of a Wall on the Occupied Palestinian Territory', 9 July 2004, General List No. 131, para. 122.

33 ibid. paras. 123-132.
34 ibid. para. 151.
35 ibid. para. 152.

of the Fourth Geneva Convention concerns the inviolability of the rights of protected persons in occupied territory, and provides that no attempt at annexation may alter the legal regime of an occupation. The official commentary to the Convention reiterates that while occupation of territory as a result of war represents actual possession to all appearances, it 'cannot imply any right whatsoever to dispose of territory',[27] and that a decision on annexation cannot be made while hostilities continue but can 'only be reached in the peace treaty'.[28]

Annexation is also in direct contravention of the rights of peoples to self-determination as set forth in Article 1 of both the ICCPR and the ICESCR. By virtue of this right peoples 'freely determine their political status and freely pursue their economic, social and cultural development'. The provision also requires each State party to the Covenants to 'promote the realization of the right to self-determination' and to 'respect that right'. In stressing its significance, the Human Rights Committee has stated that: 'The right of self-determination is of particular importance because its realization is an essential condition for the effective guarantee and observance of individual human rights and for the promotion and strengthening of those rights.'[29]

The United Nations General Assembly and Security Council have condemned Israel's de facto annexation of occupied territory in many resolutions.[30] These consistently reaffirm that the acquisition of territory by military conquest is inadmissible and reiterate the applicability of the fourth Geneva Convention to the territories under Israeli occupation. The resolutions also condemn Israel's policy of creating 'facts on the ground' in an attempt to change the legal status of the occupied areas that it has declared annexed. Israel has, however, rejected the content of these UN resolutions, and continues to defy the international community and disregard its rights and responsibilities under international law. John Dugard, the Special Rapporteur of the United Nations Commission on Human Rights to the Occupied Palestinian Territories, has affirmed that the construction of the Wall must be condemned as 'an act of unlawful annexation in the language of Security Council resolutions 478 (1980) and 497 (1981) which declare that Israel's actions aimed at the annexation of East Jerusalem and the Golan Heights are 'null and void' and should not be recognized by States'.[31]

Advisory Opinion of the International Court of Justice

In its Advisory Opinion on the Legal Consequences of the Construction of a Wall on the Occupied Palestinian Territory, delivered on 9 July 2004, the International Court of Justice held that the construction of the Wall and its associated regime are contrary to international law and an impediment of the right to self-determination,[32] as well as to freedom of movement and economic, social and cultural rights.[33] It required Israel to cease forthwith all construction, to dismantle the Wall constructed thus far[34] and to make reparations for all the damage caused by its construction in the occupied territory.[35] It held that states must not recognise the illegal situation resulting from the Wall's construction and provide neither aid nor assistance in maintaining the situation created by its construction, and that all High Contracting Parties to the fourth Geneva

Convention (which is almost every country in the world) must ensure compliance by Israel with international humanitarian law as embodied in the Convention.[36] Furthermore it required the United Nations to consider what further action is required to bring to an end the illegal situation resulting from the Wall's construction.

36   ibid. para. 146.

Conclusion

During decades of conflict with its neighbours, Egypt, Syria, Jordan and Lebanon, Israel's frontiers have fluctuated more than those of most states. Yet while each of these states has internationally recognised, if contested borders, the Palestinians remain stateless with only the pre-1967 armistice line providing a territorial reference point. In the wake of the 2006 invasion of Lebanon, Israel's deputy Prime Minister Shimon Peres wrote that 'No longer is the adage 'a people will reside alone' valid. There are no frontlines any more, in war or peace'.[37] In unilaterally imposing a border – a 'frontline' – between the Israeli and Palestinian people in the West Bank, and utterly isolating Palestinians, not only is Israel in violation of international law, but it is undermining the possibility of a peaceful negotiation to the end of this long conflict.

37   Shimon Peres, 'This war has taught us that Israel must revise its military approach', *The Guardian*, 4 September 2006.

International law provides the basis for such negotiations, premised on respect for the fundamental principles of non-discrimination, the prohibition of the threat or use of force and the right to self-determination, and to peace. The disastrous impact which can result from the fencing in and de-development of Palestinian territory has already been demonstrated in Gaza. The entire Gaza Strip, home to over a million people, is surrounded by fences and all entry and exit of goods and of people is under the control of the Israeli army. Despite total economic and military control over the population of Gaza, Israel has failed to secure peace in the area. That building walls to fence in a people deprived of the most basic human rights cannot end violence, but rather only serve to perpetuate the conflict, appears to have been dismissed in the advance to 'separate' the two peoples.

38   Question of the Violation of Human Rights in the Occupied Arab Territories, Including Palestine: Report of the Special Rapporteur of the Commission on Human Rights, Mr. John Dugard, on the situation of human rights in the Palestinian territories occupied by Israel since 1967, submitted in accordance with Commission resolutions 1993/2 A and 2002/8. E/CN.4/2003/30, 17 December 2002.

Two years after the publication of the International Court of Justice's Advisory Opinion, the construction of violence which is propelling the Annexation Wall through the West Bank continues being pursued vigorously. In a 2002 report on human rights in Palestine, the UN Special Rapporteur, John Dugard, criticised that, 'when territorial expansion occurs openly, as in the case of the purported annexation of East Jerusalem and the Golan Heights, the response of the international community, speaking through the United Nations, has been clear and firm. The response to Israel's present annexation by stealth has not, however, received the same strong condemnation'.[38] In June 2006, Dugard again raised the severe impact of the Wall's construction on human rights, highlighting the de-Palestinisation of parts of the West Bank, particularly the Jordan Valley and the South Hebron Hills, the increase in checkpoints throughout the West Bank and the forced abandonment of agricultural land in the Seam Zone as farmers are denied permits to farm their land.[39]

39   Special Rapporteur on the situation of human rights in the Occupied Palestinian Territory, Professor John Dugard, Universities of Leiden (Netherlands) and Pretoria (South Africa), 'Human Rights in Palestine', United Nations Press Release, 21 June 2006.

Construction of the Wall is accelerating the fragmentation of Palestinian society. The West Bank is completely isolated from the Gaza Strip, and the Wall, in combination with the settlement blocs, is dividing the north of the West Bank from the south, while the Seam Zone and East Jerusalem, with their large settler blocs will be de facto annexed to Israel. Should a Palestinian state be declared in the scattered remnants of the West Bank it will be little more than a Bantustan upon which Israel's military and economic designs shall be superimposed. It is unlikely that the manufacture of such an environment will assist in the struggle for peace in the Middle-East.

02.
MEM
ORY

THE SIEV X MEMORIAL PROJECT

Steve Biddulph

The Siev X Tragedy

In October 2001 a small fishing boat foundered in heavy weather, and sank in international waters, several hundred miles south of Indonesia. On board were a group of voyagers possibly unique in history. Of the roughly 160 women, 170 children, and about seventy men, 353 died, some in the sinking and some after many hours in the water. Only about forty were still alive twenty hours later, when fishing boats came across the wreckage, and at the urging of those first rescued, searched until the others had been found.[1]

The voyagers came from Iraq, and Afghanistan. They were refugees. The voyage had been organised by people smugglers, with the involvement of the Indonesian armed forces and police, and at least the knowledge of Australian secret services, who had funded a people smuggling disruption program in local ports of departure at the time. The boat, named the Siev X (from the Australian naval term SIEV for Suspect Illegal Entry Vessel) was only 19.5 metres long, and had an additional chipboard deck fitted at the last minute to carry the hugely overcrowded complement. The refugees had been terrified to see the boat, but had been assured it was to take them to a larger ship. Not all were convinced, one man trying to leave with his family had been pistol whipped and forced to stay on board.

Australian newspapers carried news of the event several days later, but in the heat of a national election campaign, the story disappeared with barely a trace.

A small group of Australians felt that their country had a responsibility in this event, the largest maritime tragedy in their region since the Second World War. Steve Biddulph, a psychologist and parenting author, Rod Horsfield, a Uniting Church minister, and Beth Gibbings, an artist and project manager, helped by many willing hands as need arose, began the Siev X National Memorial Project in 2002. They reasoned that had this tragedy involved well-off Australian or American travellers in a 747 airliner, the grief, investigations, and honouring of the dead would have been a significant and long term event. It was intrinsically racist that these refugees from the Middle East were so easily forgotten. The Government was not even willing to release their names, although somehow it had come by a complete manifest of those on the voyage. There were other reasons to feel responsible – many of the women and children were on the vessel because their menfolk had already come to Australia, and been caught up in that country's rapidly conceived detention system in remote desert or island camps, during the height of a bitterly fought election campaign involving the manipulated fear of Islamic and other outsider groups.

1   Don Greenlees, 'I have lost everything', *The Australian*, 23 October 2001.

A Dark Moment in a Dark Time

The context of the Siev X incident had some unique features embedded in the recent history and politics of the region. Australia was acting as a minor and largely symbolic ally in the 'Coalition of the Willing' in the invasion of Afghanistan and Iraq by US led forces. Independently of this a wave of refugees numbering about 4-6000 had fled from Iraq, via neighbouring Iran, over a period of several decades, and as pressure and persecution grew, they chose Australia as a friendly and welcoming destination. (Many thousands more chose other nations, and with more eventual success.) An election was taking place and in the run up to this election, the government of the day, a conservative right wing government on the Australian spectrum was widely tipped to lose. However the newly arisen fear of Islamic people in the aftermath of 9/11, and the arrival of a number of refugee vessels on Australian shores had introduced a new factor of Islamophobia into the Australian electorate, and the Government was now campaigning on a strong stand against boat people.

An extensive maritime surveillance was being carried out in the northern waters extending right up to the inshore Indonesian maritime boundaries, and several boats had been intercepted and their occupants held in essentially concentration camp conditions on offshore islands like Nauru, Christmas Island and others. Despite their legal status under the Refugee Convention, these people were not granted normal refugee status. Those who had reached Australian shores and had to be accommodated were kept in remote desert detention centres, and there were many human rights issues raised locally and from NGOs and the UN itself.

The concept of 'temporary visas' was introduced as a way to ameliorate Australia's international obligations while not giving approved refugee status to asylum seekers, and so 'caving in' to the emotional blackmail of people arriving on our shores uninvited. There were many ironies in the situation – Australia in fact was an excellent country at repatriating refugees, taking numbers in the hundreds of thousands each year without any real problems. And this wave of boat people, which became a national preoccupation for over four years and decided the electoral outcome along with many other policies, including our continued involvement in the Iraq war, numbered a mere 4000 persons in total. The asylum seekers arriving by boat did so because they came from countries that would hardly issue them with visas, or documentation, and so could not access the normal refugee channels. They were tagged as 'queue jumpers' in a context when almost any parent would have done the same thing – most did not leave their homelands until deaths or torture of family members made it obvious that it was impossible to stay. In the event, well over ninety per cent of this entire wave of boat people was found to be genuine refugees, using the most stringent criteria.[2]

2   Melissa Fyfe, 'A broken man begs to see his wife', *The Age*, 3 November 2001.

The anti-boat people measures proved successful in electoral terms, and the Government was returned. It was only after three years of widespread campaigning by human rights groups and many grassroots groups of refugee supporters that the 'race card' became unplayable, and in a subsequent election in 2004 it went unmentioned by either party. Shortly after that election, under pressure from backbenchers, and after years of fierce campaigning by church and community groups, lawyers, doctors and others, the Government released almost all parents and children from detention. Some had served up to six years and endured horrific physical and emotional harm. Children in particular who had grown up in these environments had severe developmental and psychiatric damage which would not be recoverable.

The Government argued that this was necessary to deter further waves of boat people, and thus was a humanitarian necessity. Opponents of the policy pointed out that sacrificing one group of people to save another was morally questionable, and certainly not a Christian viewpoint. And of course, the outcome, that the Siev X voyage took place at all, and that it was not rescued in spite of its departure and parlous condition being known to intelligence agencies, and its sinking not investigated fully, represents the darkest and lowest point in this whole era.

Taking Responsibility
The Siev X Memorial group felt they personally had to do something, on their own behalves, and as Australian citizens co-responsible for any action by their elected government. As the group said in an earlier publication, 'we have a responsibility – we had their husbands, but did not think about the fate of the women and children, or that they would do anything to be re-united.'[3]

The project group knew that their first task was getting people to care. Interviewed on ABC television at the fourth anniversary exhibition and memorial service, Steve Biddulph said, 'Very few people seem to know about Siev X, even fewer that it was a vessel almost entirely made up of mothers and children.' In fact we suspected that only about one in ten Australians knew the story in any kind of detail. It was this dissonance that energised us at each turn. After every screening of our documentary video, and after each event we organised, people came and told us, 'We had no idea.' Even refugee support groups and conferences were reduced to tears by the story. The challenge became to create a symbolic action which remembered an incident that few knew about in the first place. There was in Australia, always a rather protected and isolated community of white nominal Christians (although fast becoming a multicultural melting pot), a reflexive hostility to refugees, much orchestrated by the subtle inference by politicians and the press, that these strangely dressed people were really bombers and cutthroats coming here to kill and overrun us.

The key feeling among activists was a belief in the basic goodness of Australians, often documented in their response to non-threatening global disasters and in their general hospitability. (The Government knew this too, for instance it had directed all military personnel to take no 'humanizing or personalizing photographs' of refugees, which could generate sympathy or compassion.)[4] And a tame and lightweight media simply accepted the Government's refusal to admit them to any detention facility throughout the entire period. For human rights and refugee support groups, the mantra became

3 Beth Gibbings and Steve Biddulph, *Untold Tragedy: the Story of Siev X*, video transcript. 2002.

4 David Marr and Marian Wilkinson, *Dark Victory: How a Government Lied its Way to Political Triumph*, 2nd ed, Melbourne: Allen and Unwin, 2005.

5   *Amnesty International Australia: The Tiger XI Story*, www.amnesty.org.au/resources/ case_studies/the_tiger_xi, viewed on 12 June 2005.

Also: A comprehensive collection of worldwide media coverage, documentation, and debate about Siev X, has been collated by historian Marg Hutton on the award winning website www.sievx. com, viewed on 7 April 2005.

that 'if they knew the facts, their hearts would open' and in dozens of communities this actually was proven to be true. Asylum seekers once present in especially small rural communities immediately impressed locals with their friendliness, gratitude and hard working approach. A strong component of the refugee movement was based in rural Australia. A soccer team of Afghan teenage boys, many survivors of torture and the killings of their wider extended families, parents and siblings, toured the country helped by a farmer's wife, making friends and allaying the fears and projections of tens of thousands of schoolchildren.[5]

Reaching Out

The memorialising of the Siev X was set in this context of partial knowledge, mixed emotions, and slowly dawning remorse and compassion.

The group wanted to make a memorial, in a way that would involve as many Australians as possible, as befitted a disaster of this scale. Discussion with a specialist in memorial design took their thinking to a more sophisticated level. They discovered that the process of building a memorial was as important as any final structure. Memorials are about meaning, and are a physical representation of the inner processes of individuals, and their shared nature as they become part of the culture. They change the future as much as they reflect the past. This awareness made the wish to tell the Siev X story even stronger, and in fact we saw it as perhaps the heart of the whole refugee issue, for Australians to realise that lives would be endangered whenever a full-hearted response to refugee issues was not forthcoming.

The group opted to reach out to school students as a primary group for awareness raising. They represented a fresh generation. And from a remembering viewpoint, they would see the Siev X tragedy on a concrete, human level away from political and media influence as to the relative value of human lives. Thus the chances of them creating something more essential and pure and therefore powerful was greater. And that art had a definite cultural role in communicating at an emotional and symbolic level, so that no one's responses would be preconditioned; rather, each individual seeing the memorial could respond in their own way.

Every secondary school in Australia received a letter, addressed to the Art Department, inviting their participation in an Art Collaboration to design a memorial place. The only stipulation was a lakeside site, since the national capital of Australia is located on a large artificial lake, the centrepiece of that city's award-winning design. The memorial, it was felt, belonged on a shore, and at the heart of the country to which these people had hoped to make their lives. Since most Australians and in fact every school child in the country at some stage officially visits the national capital, to learn about their country's identity, the location of a memorial there seemed natural and right.

The Response

About ten per cent of the country's schools responded to request a teaching kit, and of these about 200 actual entries were received. They were often heartbreakingly poignant, and almost always showed a young person's directness of care and anger and bewilderment about the loss of the Siev X voyagers.

Among the entries were many depicting hands emerging from the water, one featured people afloat on pieces of debris, a parent and child clinging together, others floating dead on the water. Some students opted for more traditional but beautiful arrangements of 353 rose plants, trees. Sculptures both realistic and abstract. Hooded figures emerging from the water. Grieving, bereft figures gazing out to sea. A welcoming jetty, shaped like a hand with fingers extended. A rising column of children being pulled from the water by a winged angel. It was almost impossible to view the designs without being brought to tears, even for those of us who had been immersed in the facts of the tragedy for years. The public, visiting the artworks for the first time, often spent thirty or forty minutes gazing at the images and reading the descriptions by the children of what was behind their intentions.

Stephanie Yap Abidin
Tangarra School for Girls

All the artwork was archived on a website, where it can still be viewed (www. sievxmemorial.com). Exhibitions of almost all entries were held on anniversaries of the tragedy, and special services held. A particularly good outcome was that survivors and families of the dead came spontaneously to these events, and one (Amal Basry, an Iraqi mother) actually spoke to the assembled audience about the hours in the water, and some of the people who had died. It was an unforgettable moment. A year later, the same thing happened at a memorial event/exhibition in Melbourne. Fares Khadem, an Iraqi father who had lost a wife and two children on the boat, actually seeing them drown, telling them goodbye as they were torn away by waves, stepped out of the audience and told his story. His intensity of emotion seemed to be cathartic for him and our hopes for the healing power of the whole process were validated in those few minutes.

Mitchell Donaldson
Hillbrook Anglican School

The artwork process was not designated as a competition, we wanted to draw from the totality of the artworks and not create 'losers and winners'. However, from the students' art work, one particular design received acclaim from many visitors to the exhibitions, and began to form the basis of the eventual design, although many other elements were added or changed that were common to other students' work.

Tim Whitely visualised the memorial as it might look, a confronting and beautiful procession of white poles, leaving the water's edge and snaking across the land, each named for the person, adult or child, who had died.

The poles form the outline of the boat to its exact dimensions, allowing a visitor or school group to walk into the space and experience how small it was for so many people. The poles then continue in single file for almost 200 metres up a small hill. The poles which represent the graves of children are three feet high, and the ones for the adults are five feet high.

George Shehata
St Mary's Coptic Orth College

By the fourth anniversary of the Siev X tragedy, the national media showed an interest, and the head of the ACT Government (Australian Capital Territory) Chief Minister Jon Stanhope spoke in support of the project going ahead.

Moving to Completion
The process of getting the memorial in place is currently under way. The poles are adorned by a community group, school, church, or arts group who paint a band of colour and imagery to represent their part of Australia, and to celebrate and grieve for the single person their pole represents. Each pole is brought by diverse means in a journey across the continent, to be erected on the fifth anniversary in October 2006. This erection will be temporary, as a small group with limited resources we will then store the poles safely, and work with Government authorities to have them permanently set in a pathway for visitors to see over a ten-year period.

In Iraq there are already families learning of the effort of Australians to remember their loved ones, and it's anticipated that tens of thousands of people will visit the memorial and learn about the Siev X story over its lifetime. Educational material will be available for schools to learn, and many students will know of big brothers or sisters, family members or local groups who participated in making the poles.

It will be a simple, stark, haunting, peaceful but challenging reminder of the sheer loss of life, and the response of a small group of people to the challenge of remembering. It will send a contrary message to the mainstream, but one consistent with Christian, Islamic, Buddhist and humanitarian values worldwide – that every life is infinitely precious, and should be protected.

The validation of the effort and time spent on the memorial can never be fully known. Four years of our lives, and over $60,000 of our own funds went into the memorial, and it is yet to be realised. When $15,000 can fly a refugee legally and safely from Southern Sudan, this has to be assessed carefully.

It was worthwhile to simply see the first group of Islamic people – including survivors of the tragedy – walk into a Christian church – a first for all concerned – in our first event in 2003. It was worth it to see the look on a bereaved father and husband's face as he decided he would himself create the poles for his wife and daughters who had drowned on Siev X. The effect on national consciousness and resolve about better care of refugees needing our protection is part of a vast mosaic of efforts and educative work from thousands of groups and individuals; we are proud simply to be a small part of this powerful and important sea-change in our country's process of becoming a worthwhile global citizen.

SIEV X temporary memorial
building and dismantling
sequence
01

02

03

04

05

06

10

11

12

BORDERS, MEMORY AND THE SLIPPAGE IN-BETWEEN

SueAnne Ware

Introduction

This chapter discusses some of the work produced in a postgraduate design studio at the University of New Mexico in Albuquerque in late 2005. The studio was specifically framed to consider temporal memorial forms, anti-memorials, and deaths of undocumented workers crossing into the United States. The studio brief proposed contemporary anti-memorial design investigations which sought to formalise impermanence and even celebrate changing form over time and in space. Students considered multiple readings of issues relating to illegal migration: politically, socially, and physically. The examples presented in this chapter force us to reflect on our own complicity with this situation and the purposes of memory within public spaces. The project work questions the rationale behind memorial designs as an act of collective public memory and attempts to consider what I call the slippery qualities of memory and remembrance. These projects best exemplify a range of anti-memorials, as they challenge static, everlasting, conventional memorials.

El Paso/Juárez and Operation Hold the Line

In 1994 President Bill Clinton began a new border strategy; strangely enough it corresponded with the North American Free Trade Agreement (NAFTA), which supposedly sought to remove barriers between the US, Mexico, and Canada. Operation Hold the Line in El Paso, Operation Safeguard in Arizona, and Operation Gatekeeper in the San Diego area seek to effectively, physically block any possibility of immigrants crossing into the US in urban areas.[1] The US Border Patrol's blockade of the US-Mexico border in El Paso, Operation Hold the Line, was extended ten miles west along the border into southern New Mexico, in 1999. The extension of the blockade increased it to thirty miles long and the US Immigration and Naturalization Service (INS) agents currently are stationed every quarter mile along the El Paso, Texas-Ciudad Juárez border. Further, Operation Rio Grande (around Brownsville, Texas) installed thirty-one miles of floodlights along the border, prompting some environmentalists to complain that the lights harmed endangered wildlife.[2] The INS recently announced that 'There have been zero crossings by Mexicans' since the lights went up on August 26, 1997.[3] This is very much disputed. All in all it is estimated that between three and four thousand *migra*, (Immigration Agents) patrol this particular part of the border at any one time. (These include: the Immigration and Naturalization Service (INS), the National Guard (introduced recently in June 2006), and law enforcement officers from both nations in both state and federal capacities.)[4] A University of Houston study estimated that over 3000 people have died crossing the border from 1993-1999. According to records kept by the Mexican Consulate in Houston, 520 border crossers have died in Texas and New Mexico since Hold the Line began.[5]

1   US Customs and Border Protection website, http://www.cbp.gov/xp/cgov/border_security/border_patrol/overview.xml, accessed 10 June 2006.

2   Jose Palafox, http://mediafilter.org/CAQ/CAQ56border.html, 'Militarizing the border', *Covert Action Quarterly*, accessed 11 June 2006.

3   William E Clayton Jr, 'Our border can be controlled', *The Houston Chronicle*, 1 June, 1995, A15.

4   US Customs and Border Protection website, http://www.cbp.gov/xp/cgov/border_security/border_patrol/overview.xml, accessed 10 June 2006.

5   Karl Eschbach, Jacqueline Hagan, Nestor Rodríguez, Rueben Hernández-León, and Stan Bailey, 'Death at the border', *International Migration Review*, 1999, vol 33, no 2, 430-440.

Entering into Juarez / El Paso. The border is marked through the freeway and several fences

Central El Paso/Juarez city crossing, Operation Hold the Line. The border is re-enforced with three parallel fences, the Rio Grand River (in a concrete channel) and border patrol road access

Close up of the physical effects of Operation Hold the Line

One of the main consequences of Operation Hold the Line is that it has forced immigrants to cross the border in the mountains and deserts where the conditions are much harsher and more dangerous. It is estimated that over one million people per year cross illegally into the United States from Canada and Mexico mainly for the purpose of employment.[6] The city of Juárez is located on the Mexican side of the border just across from El Paso, Texas, and roughly fifteen miles from the state of New Mexico's border with Texas. Juárez, the fourth largest city in Mexico, has over two million permanent residents and an estimated half a million temporary residents. There is widespread unemployment, poverty, and homelessness in Juárez. This is partially due to the increasing number of migrants from central Mexico who come to work at the border factories (maquiladoras) as well as others who come to the border city to cross into the US illegally. There are in fact thousands of immigrants who are willing to risk their lives daily to come to work in America.

6   ibid, 437.

Fifteen kilometres east of the city, the border in open desert

Current Memorials to border crossing deaths

Most of the memorials to date are located within the Tijuana/San Ysidro border in Southern California. In 1996 President Zedillo dedicated a monument to those who *fell* trying to reach the American Dream at the Tijuana border. The marker was placed by a section of the cortend steel, two-metre-high fence at Playas de Tijuana so that during official visits the President could see it and pass by it in his motorcade. President Fox recently had this marker removed. On 2 November, 1998, migrant activists in Tijuana reminded the people of the human cost of Operation Gatekeeper. They erected wooden crosses to all those who have perished in California as a result of 'Operation Gatekeeper'. Motorists slowed traffic to a halt, while activists taped chrysanthemums to the crosses and placed small votive candles at the foot of each one. The crosses were arranged chronologically from west to east, in order of when each migrant died. The crosses were erected along a section of the border that was heavily used as a gathering point by groups of illegal migrants prior to Operation Gatekeeper. At the

7   Stop Operation Gate Keeper,
http://www.stopgatekeeper.org,
accessed 7 May 2006.

western end of the boulevard, a traffic island was converted to a shrine to the dead migrants, with flowers, offerings of food, and even money placed at the foot of a cross tied to a eucalyptus tree.[7] Numerous memorial remembrance days have also been organised by local churches and non-profit organisations on both sides of the border. Along Boulevard Aeropuerto there is a more permanent, spontaneous memorial.

This memorial, which includes white painted crosses and decorated coffins, follows the fence, *la linea*, for about two miles. It has both crosses which are left blank for those who were never identified, *no identifacado*, and crosses with the first names of those who have died, their age, and the state they were from. Seen from a moving vehicle, the names seem to flick through the air one by one, like ghosts. In Holtville, California, located in the Imperial Valley, 120 miles east of San Diego on Interstate eight, there is a cemetery with over 400 grave markers. Many of them are anonymous, Jane and John Doe migrants.

8   *Red* states and *Blue* states
refer to those US states whose
residents predominantly voted
for the Republican Party or
Democratic Party, respectively,
in US elections, especially in
the US presidential elections
of 2000 and 2004. Only three
states (New Mexico, Iowa, and
New Hampshire) shifted parties
between these two elections. In
the latter contest, thirty-one US
states were *Red* and nineteen
states were *Blue*, though twelve
of those *Red* states were *Blue* as
recently as 1996.

In the other border states Arizona, New Mexico, and Texas there are no official memorial sites. There are numerous spontaneous memorials but it is difficult to tell whether they mark undocumented workers deaths or if they are typical roadside memorials. On the Mexican side of the border, mainly in Nogales, there are similar memorials to the spontaneous ones found in Tijuana. Juárez has neither official nor spontaneous memorials marking the deaths of undocumented workers trying to cross over through and around El Paso, Texas. Perhaps the lack of official memorials outside of California occurs because, unlike southern California's relatively liberal political attitudes, Texas and New Mexico are archly conservative, *Red* states.[8] And while even the deeply traditional, rural communities of New Mexico harbor much resentment towards illegal migrants, they recognise the need for them within their own agricultural labour forces. It is estimated that up to seventy per cent of the agricultural economy

Coffin memorial at Tijuana Airport entrance and exit. Each has the date and number of dead found within the San Ysidro/Tijuana border area

Permanent memorial crosses at
Tijuana's Airport Boulevard

Close up of memorial anonymous
markers in Holtville

Holtville cemetery and memorial
to undocumented workers

9 The Migration Policy Institute, http://www.migrationinformation. org/feature/display.cfm, accessed July 14 2006.

of Texas and New Mexico is reliant upon undocumented workers' efforts.[9] It behoves the economies of both states to support safe entry into America for these workers. The proposed memorials which follow wrestle with many of the conundrums facing notions of borders be they political, social, or economic.

Design Proposals

> The United states is in the throes of a memorial mania that manifests itself in two ways. First, memorials culminate every conflict, act, notable death, or historical moment. The have become the morbid cigarette we consume after tragedy, as if every loss remains somehow incomplete without its permanent place in the public sphere, in spite of the fact that the nature of the public becomes increasingly ambiguous. Second, memorials have succumbed to the forces of multiculturalism and political correctness, and like the pluralistic-some would say balkanised – society they represent, they have become cauliflowers, each one reflecting the messy aggregation of interests of democracy trafficking in official remembrance.[10]

10 Andrew M Shanken, 'Memento more: Putting the new wave of memorials into context', *Frameworks*, no 2, vol Fall 2005, 3 – 11, 3.

Andrew Shanken's sentiment summarises contemporary dilemmas in memorial making and helps to position much of what the following investigations into temporary and ephemeral memorials or *anti-memorials* tries to resist. Perhaps in speculating that memory can fade and even die, the investigation of anti-memorials in this context brought about a range of potential design gestures. The following student work interrogates memorials as well as borders. It utilises design research to frame a range of contemporary political and social issues as well as proposes formal, spatial design investigations.

Mariposa and Miagra

11 Shaffee Wilson-Jones, competition submission, November 2005.

Shaffee Jones-Wilson's proposal involves creating habitat for endangered migrant butterflies as a system of marking or wayfinding in desert environs for undocumented workers. Shaffee's proposal in the Vamori Wash of the Arizona desert utilises native plant species of chamisa, milkweed and aster blossom in nectar corridors.[11] These corridors support the seasonal migration patterns of monarch butterflies from northern states in America deep into Mexico. They are also directional, the plantings operating in a north-south axis which guides migrant workers along drainage corridors to safety. She cleverly placed the corridors as physical, spatial locators in an otherwise open, disorientating desert field. There is also another layer of folklore and symbolism in selecting the monarchs as they are *mariposa* or symbols in Mexican culture of departed souls. The monarch butterflies return to Mexico during Day of the Dead celebrations in late October and early November; this coincides with migrant workers coming into America to harvest a multiplicity of crops. The serendipity of seasonal travel or migration past an arbitrary political boundary but via an ecological, biological boundary constitutes a deeper engagement with this project beyond its poetics. Human relocation patterns aside, as they will be discussed at length in the next project, this proposal links biophysical corridors, growth habitats, drainage and ephemeral creeks as a subversive strategy for safe passage. Critically, one might ask, as a few critics have, is this responsible? Should we really be encouraging 'safe' passage through hostile, arid environments? Does this proposal not accept the inevitability of border enforcement in safer areas to cross? How is it really commemorating those who have perished through illegally crossing the border? What is interesting about this proposition is that instead of solemnly saluting those who have lost their lives crossing the border, it offers hope. It uses landscape and its inherent properties as a program for a literal and figurative living memorial. The biome or program of landscape itself, water drainage, plant growth, nectar production, is reconsidered as a territorial marking, a set of directional vectors. The designer layers an ethno-botanical or cultural reading of a natural phenomena into a challenging contemporary context. She uses a romanticised symbol of the past to incite criticism of contemporary practices. This proposition in its simplicity forces us to reconsider the value of habitat reconstruction beyond its inherent ecological value into a more human ecology. It recognises that flora and fauna do not respect political boundaries and that society willingly accepts this, so why should humans?

Border Stories
Genieve Sanchez's project proposes that the freeway experience becomes a memorial journey. A series of mnemonic devices recognises those who have lost their lives illegally crossing the border. Geneive's work utilises narrative, a common device in landscape design, in a richly layered, contemporary manner. She proposes to literally infect the drive from El Paso/Juárez to Sante-Fe, New Mexico along Interstate twenty-five with memorial moments. Her work utilises both personal narratives from undocumented Mexican migrants and statistical quantities in the context of the everyday road journey. For example, she proposes adding the number of footsteps it may take to reach various locations alongside the mileage on official road signs. Rest stops have messages about the amount of water necessary to walk through the desert to remain alive, tourist radio information stations play migrant workers songs and poetry, mobile phones blink with text messages reminding us of the number of dead, billboards advertise the migrant worker who picked your produce, even your trip to the gas station is invaded as you fill your car with gasoline, the number of migrant deaths ticks over, just as the number of gallons does. The project draws from contemporary artists Sophie Calle's and Barbra Krueger's practice in the everyday realm. However, Geneive takes a uniquely disturbing approach in that she finds the places which are allocated for respite and rest along a road journey and rudely interrupts them. Just when the traveler takes a breather or is lulled by the journey, she reminds them of the consequences of America's economic democracy. Her statistics alongside the mundane ones of the road journey force us to reflect on our consumption patterns and the consequences of capitalist production. She comments critically on our passivity and complacency and perhaps our blind eye towards the practices which result in undocumented workers' deaths to begin with. The work does so in an overt and literal manner but without an accusation. The personal accounts humanise the numbers, the statistics force us to understand the magnitude of this issue.

If the previous project draws upon the poetry of Mexican folklore, this project draws upon a twentieth-century phenomena, the road journey. They both have mythical status, but it is the road trip in particular in America's Southwest. Geneive's work

Genieve Sanchez's proposals for Border Stories

12 James E Young, 'Germany's holocaust memorial problem – and mine', *The Public Historian*, vol 24, no 4, Fall 2002, 65-80.

13 Brett Milligan, competition submission, November 2005.

taps into all things Route 66 and shifts the celebrated freedom of a car journey into a political indictment. She forces us to consider the price we and others pay for how we live our everyday lives. Is this work too confrontational? Will it create the expected political correctness and a backlash of liberal versus conservative rhetoric? Is its literal narrative, just another attempt into shocking us? If the journey is taken more than once does it lose its effectiveness? Can the American and Mexican public really accept this as a mournful symbol of lives tragically lost or is it merely a clever campaign? Whatever the response is to this type of approach to memorialisation, it does in fact stimulate discussion and debate. James Young asserts that perhaps it is not about the actual memorial objects or spaces but the deliberations and examinations which precede it and occur as a result of memory work which constitutes the true memorial.[12]

Inundating the Border: Migratory Spaces Within the Seam

Brett Milligan's proposal examines the physical space of the border. He researched the continual re-configuration of the border area between El Paso and Juárez since the Mexican Cession of 1848, the Treaty of Guadalupe-Hidalgo, and the Gadsden Purchase in 1853, established the border's inception over 150 years ago.

Historically and legally, the border is marked by the Rio Grande/Rio Bravo del Norte River. As it is a meandering river, the international border migrated for a number of years within the ebb and flow of the water and its riparian ecosystem. The Chamizal Dispute, a border dispute lasting over 100 years between the United States and Mexico, was caused by the natural change of course of the river between the cities of El Paso and Juárez, Chihuahua. A national memorial was established on part of the disputed land that was assigned to the United States according to the Chamizal Treaty of 1963; a corresponding Parque Público Federal 'El Chamizal' was created on the now-Mexican portion of the land. The river was stabilised within a concrete channel. This change left a void in the urban fabric, the empty parkland, between Juárez and El Paso that still exists today.[13] Brett's project examines what could occur if the river was de-channelised and allowed to inundate and fluctuate once again. The physical border becomes blurred through various entopic landscape processes. In a practical sense the site can now accommodate surface water run-off and mitigate flash flooding which has resulted from the rapid urbanisation of Juárez/El Paso. Further Brett writes,

> The Rio Grande/Rio Bravo is a polluted and dying river. Regulated flows and concrete channels engineered in the 1960s have eliminated much of the riparian habitat along its banks. Industries on both sides of the border dump heavy metals, and runoff from irrigated fields increases the alkalinity of the water. If the Rio Grande is released from the concrete channel, it will once again penetrate into the ground, and create a diversity of habitats, such as bosques, meadows and wetlands that will begin to reclaim the river through regenerative natural processes. These environments will emerge and migrate with the fluctuations of the river, creating places that are never the same. An abandoned braid of the river becomes a tall grass meadow...the next day the river floods and the meadow lies beneath the swiftly moving current. Years later riparian trees have matured and the place becomes a shady bosque. During a particularly dry year, the space becomes part of the border patrol surveillance pathways...

MIGRANT DEATHS & MONARCH FLIGHT PATHS

Seattle
New York
Albuquerque
Los Angeles Phoenix
Tucson
Mexico City

NORTHERN HABITAT
April-August

March- April

September- November

December- March
SOUTHERN HABITAT

tree canopy

understory

ground covers

Monarch butterfly sanctuaries
MEXICO
Ciudad Hidalgo
SIERRA CHINCUA
Angangueo
ROSARIO
Zitacuaro
Other protected areas
MICHOACAN
MILES 20

MEXICO
MICHOACAN
Gulf of Mexico
Detail area
Mexico City
Pacific Ocean
New York Times Graphic

Deforestation Surrounding Sanctuary
Rosario Butterfly Sanctuary
Monarchs In Flight

Body Collection
Gift Creation
Traveling Memorial
Reforesting
Planted North- South axis to honor migration

Monarch bodies collected each season and fashioned into purchaseables to be sold abroad.

Employees, former farmers, replant trees and collect seeds for Monarch Waystation Seed Kits. These are sold in the US. They are also given to migrants by family members, a traveling memorial, to disburse on their travels and at the memorial site for nectar coordor establishment.

Funds support local economy, artisans and reforesting program including employment of farmers.

A Memorial to Those Who Have Died Crossing

In barren desert cooridors across the Mexico and US border, native plant species are planted to provide food for the migrating Monarch butterfly. The Monarch's treacherous journey echoes those made by desperate migrant workers.

The designed conservation corridor is placed at Vamori Wash. The greatest number of human deaths and monarch sightings have been documented at this location.

By using this beacon of chamisa, milkweed and aster, both types of migrant, human and butterfly, find their way through the desert. In this way, these growing beacons sustain life, prevent death and memorialize those who have died crossing.

BORDER STORIES

US INTERSTATE 25: NEW MEXICO

THIS IS A SOCIAL AND ECONOMIC PROBLEM THAT REQUIRES ECONOMIC AND SOCIAL CHANGE

"I DISGUISED MYSELF AS AN ANGLO AND DYED MY HAIR BLOND."

CALIFORNIA, NEW YORK, TEXAS & FLORIDA CONTAIN THE LARGEST % OF ILLEGAL IMMIGRANTS

"THEY CARRIED CRACKERS, CORN CHIPS & TORTILLAS TO SUSTAIN THEM. IT WAS HARDLY ENOUGH"

IMMIGRANT DEATHS INCREASE YEARLY ON A REGULAR BASIS

A GALLON OF WATER WEIGHS 8.5 LBS AND CAN LAST THAN LESS THAN A DAY

"THE DANGER OF THE AMERICAN INTERVENTION"

EXHAUSTION, DEHYDRATION, OVERHEATING & ASPHYXIATION STARTS WHEN BODY TEMPERATURES REACH 107 DEGREES

THE ONION WILL ROT, SO TO THE CROPS TOO, BECAUSE IF THEY DEPORT THE WETBACK WHO WILL WORK

THE DESERT FLOOR CAN REACH 160 DEGREES IN THE SUMMER

MEXICO HAS A JOB DEFICIT OF 20%

THE BORDER PATROL DOES NOT BOTHER US WHEN WE ARE WORKING

AND HERE I STILL REMAIN, COUNTRYMEN, IRRIGATING THE FIELDS, WITH...

THIS IS THE STORY OF THE POOR WHO FLEE ONLY TO HAVE HERE

"THE IMMIGRATION CAUGHT ME, 300 TIMES, LET US SAY, BUT THEY NEVER BROKE ME DOWN"

Border Cross Section

Water occupation

time   ecologies   water   infrastructure   people

People occupation

Fluctuation

Indeterminacy

Entropy

How can the U.S -- Mexico border be designed as a migratory space that constantly shifts through time and events...a space composed of ephemeral moments that change from one day to the next...

El Paso, United States

Ciudad Juarez, Mexico

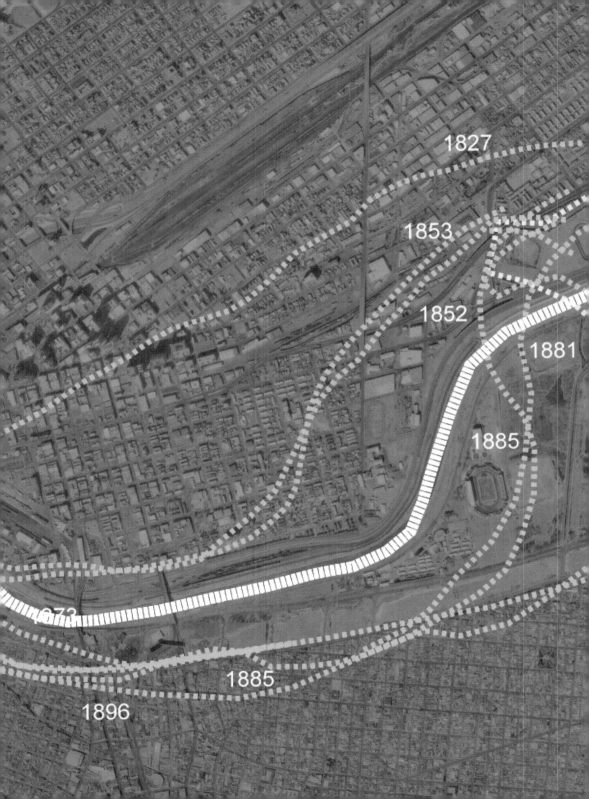

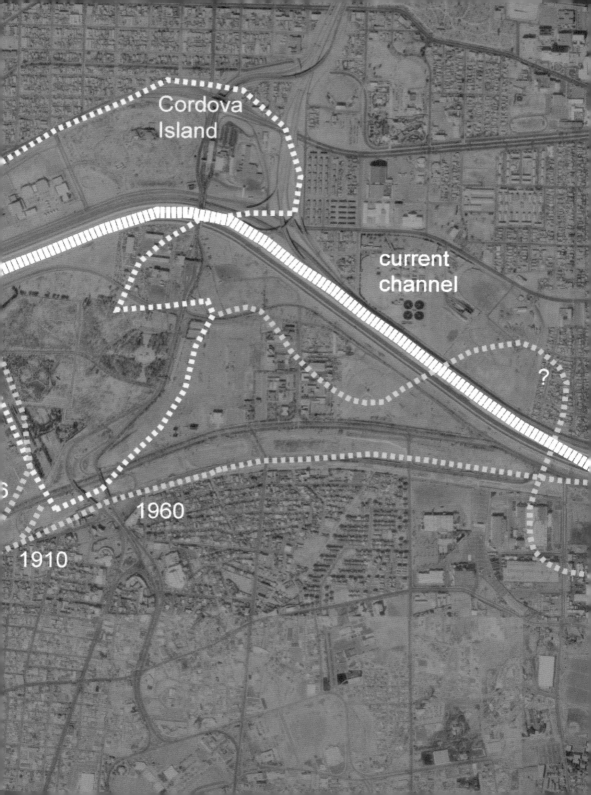

His design work speculates on fluctuation and emergence beyond the landscape's ecological systems through a series of proposed public occupations. He sites temporary festivals and events carnivals during drier months, provides for temporary shelters for homeless or migrant workers passing through, and areas for conventional riverside activities such as fishing, walking, and sitting. He does not deny that the political border exists as he provides various access points and roads for the border patrol, but they constantly shift with the changes in the landscape. There is both a convergence of site, politics, and landscape ephemera and a divergence in the strict delineation of the border. The border is recognised as a thickness which recedes and expands because of a variety of forces. It is celebrated as indeterminate and its own potential space.

This project forces us to concede that the border is not merely a line on a map or a political boundary. It is a unique spatial entity. Brett utilises a somewhat conventional approach or perhaps better stated he presents a very landscape architectural exploration of the possibilities of border spaces. His work is situated well within contemporary design examinations of open systems and dynamic processes. And while it may be reminiscent of James Corner's and Field Operation's proposals for the Fresh Kills Landfill site or Downsview Park, he positions the political border as paramount not subservient to the landscape operations. It is an intertwining of systems, a palimpsest which engages the physical landscape context and the economic phenomena of border cities. There is a dense weaving of ecological programs, public events culture, urban and environmental infrastructure, public space, border security and surveillance coming together and converging here. His work invests in and celebrates the possibilities of a border condition.

Comparatively, Brett's and Shaffee's works consider critically landscape conditions; they are not memorials in the conventional sense. They explore the possibilities and specificities of site and landscape operations. They do not necessarily ignore the tragedies; they search for alternatives to current socio-political conditions rather than literally mourn the dead. One critic astutely observed that they designed spaces which occur after the grieving; they get on with life.[14] Their work allows for a diversity of experience and definition in commemoration practice. Geneive's project is perhaps a more direct anti-memorial, she wants us to understand the gravity of the situation. She interrupts our journey and asks for compassion. She accepts and twists what Shaken writes, 'All memorials are forms of media and modes of propaganda…'[15] She uses the medium of consumption and transportation to critique human costs for the American way of life. It is both poignant and political.

Andreas Huyssen writes, 'Remembrance as a vital human activity shapes our links to the past, and the ways we remember define us in the present. As individuals and societies, we need the past to construct and to anchor our identities and to nurture a vision of the future.'[16] How then do we consider the abstruse qualities of memory and remembrance? Memory is always affected by a complex spectrum of states and stimuli such as forgetting, denial, repression, trauma, recounting, reconsidering, changes in context and changes over time. If memory is not some sort of platonic ideal that is pure or complete, but a periodic process of re-evaluation and reconstruction given present contexts, our ideas about designing memorials should evolve accordingly. There is an incongruity between the inherent changeability of landscapes and memories and conventional formal strategies of commemoration. Memory tends to be fading, shifting, fleeting, and the landscape is constantly evolving and emerging;

14 Elizabeth Boults, assessment panel, November 2005, Albuquerque, NM.

15 op cit, Shanken, 5.

16 Andreas Huyssen, 'Monument and memory in a postmodern age', in James Young (ed), The Art of Memory: Holocaust Memorials in History, New York: The Jewish Museum, 1994, 9-17.

the design work presented in this chapter takes this into consideration. James Young writes that public memory is constructed, that understanding events depends on memory's construction. He suggest that memory must undergo continual renewal in order for the subject of remembrance, in this instance the deaths of undocumented workers traveling into the US illegally, to stay vivid in our collective conscious.[17] The memory work presented here hopes to illicit discussion and renewal of this ongoing debate.

17   James E Young, *The Texture of Memory: Holocaust Memorials and Meaning*, New Haven, CT: Yale University Press, 1993, 39.

Beyond grappling with temporary or ephemeral memorials, or anti-memorials, the work presented here engages in a kind of design activism. The design work proposes physical catalysts for social change. Harrison Fraker writes:

> Design Activism is problem seeking, it is proactive, it chooses an issue (or set of issues) and explores it (or them) from a critical, sometimes ideological perspective. It uses design to recognise latent potential and make it visible. It explores 'absences' in everyday life and gives them a 'presence.' It reveals new ways of seeing the world and challenges existing paradigms.[18]

18   Harrison Fraker, 'Message from the Dean, The College of Environmental Design at the University of California at Berkeley', *Frameworks*, issue 1, Spring 2005, CED, Berkeley, CA, 3.

The life-worlds of those affected by these tragedies and the everyday context of the public realm are significant settings for these attempts to bring about change. It is in these lived, familiar spaces that we can begin to empathise with and grasp the realities of what others maybe feeling. We see that our worlds are not so different from their worlds, and that we share the same places in our cities, on our roads, and in our communal spaces. The resolve of the work to comment on issues within contemporary society is vital to its effectiveness. However, the work also speculates beyond comment or concerns into challenging ideas about international borders and their static nature. Landscape is vital in this sense in that it is both emergent and a complex political entity. It offers ideas about democratic space and a public realm that embody certain types of social, environmental, and cultural responsibilities.

After the completion of the studio in late November 2005, a number of events occurred to make this work even more poignant. In early January 2006 US Congressional battles began and continue to rage on about issuing temporary day labour visas or guest worker programs for Mexican migrant workers. An anti-*illegal aliens'* citizens group, the Minutemen Militia, began a series of public demonstrations, civil actions, and personal attacks on undocumented workers. They continue to use various types of intimidation tactics to scare and harass those who they feel are in the US illegally. The often photograph groups of day labourers and report them to immigration officials and the border patrol.[19]   In June 2006 President Bush posted 6000 additional National Guards troops along the US/Mexican border. He proclaimed, 'Our whole message here is we are not at war. Mexico is our good friend to the south,' adding later, 'What we want the public to know is we do not have an enemy here. These immigrants are not our enemy. This is not about these people. It's about national security.'[20] Bush's policy and subsequent actions are not without critics. In a moving day of national action, in cities all over America and in Mexico, an estimated three million people participated in street marches, purchase bans, and work walk outs. Dubbed A Day without Immigrants, 1 May 2006 was recorded as one of the largest political protests in America since the Vietnam war.[21]   *Today we march, tomorrow we vote!*

19   The Minutemen Civil Defense Corps, http://www.minutemanhq. com/bf/ , accessed July 5 2006.

20   Daniel Gonzalez, 'Bush's 1st support wave freeing up Border Patrol', *The Arizona Republic*, 24 June 2006, 1, col 1.

21   Jill Serjeant, 'US migrants down tools in bid to gain rights for illegals', *The Age*, 3 May 2006, 4.

03.

TEM
PO
RAL
ITY

SUPERNATURAL

José Parral

Urban Fluctuations and the Alter Ego of Self and Planned Organisations
Upon entering one of the disciplines of architecture, landscape architecture, urban design or planning, you typically have the drive to solve problems and use your capabilities to change the world for the better good. Those same qualities can be compared to a comic superhero. The supernatural traits of a superhero could extend out to a city's abilities and potential, in particular its infrastructure. For example, the amount of effort and energy it takes to create highway systems for the efficiency of circulation could potentially incorporate other functions or programs, such as housing, markets, emergency shelters etc. Cities and designers embody these supernatural tendencies that are ready and waiting to be discovered.

Like Superman, the cities of San Diego and Tijuana and their urban organisations possess both the qualities of Superman and his alter ego Clark Kent. How can we begin to learn from the two cities and be able to create new assemblages of an urban fabric that could at some moments act subtle and at others have the ability to deal with extreme conditions? Superman might show us clues as to how cities have the capability to deal with extreme conditions.

During the early 1940s, Fleischer studios produced nine cartoons based on the comic book hero Superman.[1] There are two aspects of these cartoons that are interesting when compared to city organisation. The first is the superhero Superman, a being arriving to earth from a distant planet. Born from the planet Krypton, Superman embodies out of this world abilities due to his genetic make-up, 'Faster than a speeding bullet! More powerful than a locomotive! Able to leap tall buildings in a single bound'![2] When Superman is placed in the context of planet earth, the discovery of his supernatural capabilities shows a potential in dealing with extreme conditions. We also have Clark Kent, the mild-mannered reporter who is able to blend in with others who are not supernatural. This assimilation becomes critical in dealing with everyday conditions not only for the Superman character, but also with the environment of cities not exhausting energy and resources consistently. The second aspect is the cartoon storylines. In the Fleischer version of the Superman series, Superman is battling extremes with both natural catastrophes as in the cartoon Volcano and human destruction in The Mechanical Monsters, where robots invade the city robbing banks. These circumstances could be compared to warfare and natural disasters occurring to our cities today. Extreme measures call for an extreme reaction. Can planners and designers begin to investigate how cities intrinsically possess this spectrum of abilities from the banal to emergency, and develop a recourse for the implementation of designing or reconstructing urban regions confronting serious issues?

1   Wikipedia, 'Superman (1940s cartoons)', http://en.wikipedia.org/wiki/Superman_ (1940s_cartoons), viewed on 21 June 2005

2   op cit.

San Diego and Tijuana/Clark Kent and Superman

At first glance we can compare San Diego with Clark Kent and Tijuana with Superman, in relation to how each city performs to changing conditions. However, upon further investigation, there is no difference in kind, but rather degrees of these Superman/Clark Kent tendencies. Cities are naturally made up of these tendencies. In Rem Koolhaas' investigation of Lagos, the urban environment reacts to the ideal 1970s urban planning, even though at first glance it might appear as an unorganised condition. The planning for Lagos did not anticipate the population explosion or the economic dive that it has taken over the past thirty years. However, at a closer look, a fluctuating urbanism emerges, reacting to the planned/constructed conditions. Self-organisation becomes evident in the availability of open spaces that the city provides in speeds of various movements. Koolhaas immediately discovered the people of Lagos needed to use their intuition and intelligence in reacting to these urban conditions. In his investigations, Koolhaas discusses that however good or bad planning is, it is an important mix for the city, and planning will become a critical ingredient to the development of Lagos as it will develop into the largest city in the world by the year 2020.[3] Koolhaas' investigation of Lagos shares the dual traits of Superman (self-organisation) and Clark Kent (planning of the city). The following is some information that reveals San Diego's characteristics and abilities that begin to show the commonality between the character of Superman/Clark Kent described earlier.

The city of San Diego shares some of the same qualities as our character Clark Kent, with its conformity to the rest of the region of Southern California. The climate is one condition that cannot be controlled. However, it does not matter; the change in weather is subtle, averaging between seventy-seven degrees Fahrenheit and forty-nine degrees Fahrenheit (twenty-five degrees Celsius to nine degrees Celsius) over the year. The climate only reinforces San Diego's relaxed quality of life. There are more people over the age of sixty-five living in San Diego than the city of Miami, which is typically know as a place of retirement. San Diego's infrastructure shares the same traits as Clark Kent, highly efficient and never straying from the goal, resulting in an inflexible linear system. The high level of bureaucratic order makes it difficult for any difference to emerge and affects the possibility for alternatives in urban form. Before we can begin to provide a difference, codes and laws need to change. For example, to proceed with designing a property with denser housing, architect Teddy Cruz had to go through a process which took five years to change San Diego's zoning laws.[7] The rigidity of this organisation, formal or otherwise, is reinforced by economic tension. You have to double your income to afford a median priced house. San Diego is becoming more and more exclusive.

Upon further investigation, there are also traits that are similar to Superman's abilities that could be tapped as a resource. One of San Diego's strengths (if one can have access to it) is in its economic makeup. Its biotechnology community is the third largest in the country. San Diego's communications industry is one of the fastest growing in the country and has earned it the title of wireless communications capital

3   Bregtje van der Haak and Rem Koolhaas, 'Lagos wide and close an interactive journey into an exploding city', 120 minutes DVD, Submarine, 2005.

San Diego data:
1. San Diego has 1,305,736 residents, the seventh largest metropolitan area in the United States and is home to many military facilities.[4]
2. The population of residences over sixty-five years old in San Diego County is ranked fourth, one higher from Miami-dale County based on the 2000 census.[5]
3. The median priced house is US$550,000 (~AUS$713,711) and the median household income of US$64,273 (~AUS$83,406).[6]

4   United States. US Census Bureau.United States Census 2000. CA: US Census Bureau, 2001.

5   op cit.

6 San Diego Housing Commission, 'San Diego's housing crisis – statistics and quotes', http://www.sdhc.net/giaboutus2.shtml, viewed on 3 March 2006.

7   Nicolail Ouroussoff, 'Shantytowns as a new suburban ideal,' New York Times, 12 March 2006.

of the world. San Diego has been marked one of the six centers of innovation.[8] In order for the city to survive in relation to cost of living, it needs to provide a space where innovation can occur. The relationship between the University of California San Diego and the various private biotech and communication enterprises offers the possibilities for innovation to happen in many different ways. This condition is much like the ones described by De Landa in A Thousand Years of Nonlinear History. For instance, the development of Silicon Valley, where institutions and industries create a symbiotic relationship relying on local knowledge to promote innovation and creating difference for alternative urban form.[9]

Tijuana performs similar to Superman in its ability to continually solve potential disasters from a multitude of self-organised situations. For instance, small markets emerge while waiting to cross the border into California. Vendors are always looking for opportunities to sell. Conditions created by mass-produced housing due to lack of enforcing codes allow people to adapt to their environments, for example, room additions for extended family, use of home as a store front, ranging from mechanic shops to the selling of goods to food stands. The people of Tijuana are always redefining architecture, landscape and urbanity, due to lack of code and law enforcement in relation to land development by its segregated economy. Tijuana's people and urbanism are using all of the necessary power and strength to find the path of least resistance to simply survive, a path towards opportunity (economic, social, and political). With that in mind, continual daily struggles and the city's makeup are constantly moving to solve a multitude of problems, living many times over a day in a Superman episode. As a design theory, Tijuana becomes an example of a supernatural because of its dynamic organisations and constant resource for innovation and theorising.

When looking at Tijuana more closely, its fluctuating urbanism hardly functions. And because of its lack of efficiency, it begins to cause more problems and the quality of life diminishes. For example, when squatters occupy portions of land, this causes instability with poor construction and lack of planning for stormwater management, resulting in the intensification of mudslides during seasonal storms and contamination of the water system. This is multiplied many times over throughout the city. Furthermore, the intensity of crime due to the lack of enforcement and much corruption clearly creates an unsafe environment. This clearly shows that Tijuana's organisation needs an aptitude for dealing with the dangers of everyday living and requires the people to have a supernatural resistance. As a result, safety and security are critical necessities.

What physically defines the different cultures between San Diego and Tijuana is the border fence causing specialisation, similarly to the process of the Galapagos Islands. This becomes an opportunity for research of not just one design strategy versus the other, but also of how designers and planners begin to look at these two cities and evaluate, measure, and speculate alternative urbanisms by combining both. If we were to embody the composite of Superman/Clark Kent, combinations of hierarchical and network urban layouts become necessary. Government policies need to be more

8 'A thriving economy', San Diego Regional Economic Development Corp, April 27 2006. http://www.sandiegobusiness.org/economy.asp 27 April 2006, viewed on 27 April, 2006.

9 Manuel De Landa, A Thousand Years of Nonlinear History, New York: Swerve, 1997, 95-97.

Tijuana data:
1. Tijuana's population is 1,210,820 and a density of 2212 hab/km², nearly double when compared to San Diego with 1,456.4hab/km².[10]
2. Tijuana had 396 homicides in 2005, up 355 from the previous year.[11]

10 'Enciclopedia de los Municipios de México', TIJUANA, 2002, Instituto Nacional para el Federalismo y el Desarrollo Municipal, http://www.e-local.gob.mx/work/templates/enciclo/bajacalifornia//, viewed on 24 April, 2006.

11 Sandra Dibble, 'Tijuana takes high-tech road to combat crime', San Diego Tribune, 16 February 2006, http://www.signonsandiego.com/news/mexico/tijuana/20060216-9999-7m16tjtour.html, viewed on 25 April, 2006.

Vendors at La Linea

12   op cit. 80-83.

sensitive to opportunities, issues and changes that occur over time. Self-organisation creates opportunities and problems, and these policies would need to develop management guidelines and find solutions that adapt to conditions and, at the same time, prevent dangerous situations. De Landa also describes the combination of these two types of organisations as always being in existence.[12] The challenge would be in how to understand these relationships and test alternative urban models.

Jardines Playas de Tijuana/La Esquina

In 2003 through 2005 I had the privilege to work with InSite and an artist to create a permanent art piece/infrastructural project on the most north-western corner of Mexico. This was an attempt to inject an urbanism with supernatural qualities.

While investigating the city of Tijuana, particularly the area of Las Playas de Tijuana, we began to build up an ambitious drive to incorporate non-traditional systems that would adapt and work with flexibility. In addition, we were to work within the conditions of a landscape/art project.

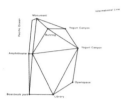

Openspace Network

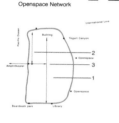

Openspace Loop

Masterplan, the Las Playas area

Our strategy for this project was to work at two scales. The large scale quasi-master plan was for most of the north-western zone of Las Playas. It extends from the Mexico/US border to further south, the first series of public parks, library (small and for children's parties) down from Torreo, and east to the first ravine that outputs northward to the United States. This large scale project established a network of social, economical, and environmental links that attempted to show a seamless connection between the various urban nodes. Criteria of performances (fitness, commerce, eco flow patterns, and social activities) would perform as a model for the organisation of the various connections. The zone negotiations between the various private owners could establish new fields. For example, the Bullring parking lot could be an opportunity for change, and this could become a benefit for the owner, local residents, vendors and visitors.

At a smaller scale, the project became an urban restratification that kept in mind social, economical and environmental factors, and at the same time, recorded our investigation and development. The project is located at the fence of Las Playas, from the Bullring and Lighthouse to the ocean. This area, in particular, is one of extremes and dualities: land to water, third to first world, urban to natural, construction to decay. Within these dualities, we wanted to create a condition that would consider all of these extremities and produce new ones. We also saw opportunity within the contextual situation and its physical makeup: the strolling locals and tourists, beachfront hangout, fishermen, water enthusiasts, coconut vendors, fence observation point, topographic variances, vista of the estuary to the north and use as a meeting point in Tijuana. The intervention by participants blurred boundaries between landscape, architecture and art, and expanded the connection of all these fields. Due to the limited expansion of both Tijuana and San Diego in the north, east and south directions, the west can be imagined as a new vector for a free exchange of the two regions. The project will ultimately provide a bridge between the past (existing conditions) and the possibility of an open future (the ocean).

Jardines Playas de Tijuana/La Esquina

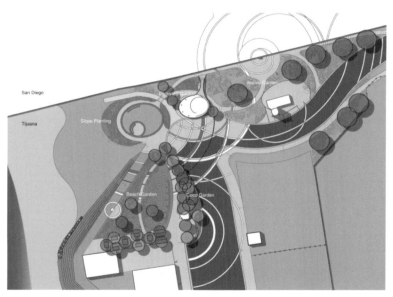

Site plan

Native Garden
A collection of native plants to act as an demonstration of various species native to the area. The attempt will also provide a connection to of plants to the park on the side of San Diego

Coco Garden
The coconut vender was moved to a new location in the final plan. A garden was created to reinforce the tropical attitude

Backyard Garden
The plants in this would be what you would typical see in the residences of Tijuana.

Beach Garden
The beach garden uses bands of color (from blues, and violets to yellows and reds) to provide a graphic facing the ocean and areas up above. The plant material is what is normally seen the beach environment along the coast of both countries.

Slope Garden
A combination of native grasses and other plant material to retain the slope and cactuses to prevent people from walking along the slope.

At a more fundamental level, we layered new sediment that performed its most basic function as a series of circulation patterns for pedestrians, wheelbarrows, carts and vehicles. At the same time, we forced new material organisation to serve other potentials: blocking wind, providing shade, and preventing slope erosion. And we incorporated programs: the lighthouse, symbolic relationships of the monuments, the showers and bathrooms, the coconut vendor and a public plaza.

Throughout the process, everyone had to overcome numerous challenges, including negotiating the building process of the park land with various city and community organisations, obtaining the necessary resources to prevent further soil erosion, limiting vehicular traffic, improving basic services, and above all, engendering new sustainable patterns of growth and urban re-organisation, while respecting Tijuana's natural and constructed surroundings. In a fundamental sense, the project naturally inherited the qualities of the Superman and Clark Kent model. A major part of these qualities arose from the collaboration between Thomas Glassford and myself, as well as the requests from others who had participated, and the construction process itself. As a result, a strange juxtaposition of an appealing landscape with the contextual conditions of Las Playas occured. In the region's incessant change the contrasts will blend further. We merely provided reorganisation for a new starting point that will offer layers of intervention.

Why create alternative urban organisations? Again, I would look at Superman/Clark Kent as a model. Natural disasters or destruction caused by warfare begin to bring up issues of rebuilding and prevention. It also becomes an opportunity to re-strategise. Can we formulate alternative strategies that address the prevention of loss and create comfortable places for people to live and develop? This supernatural urbanism would have to be a fabricated history, just like the story of Superman, but in the end possess the ability to react quickly to disasters. It would also show us alternatives by looking at the city in the same way one would go to Tijuana and discover something new everyday.

The workshop in Mexico City provided the milieu to begin cataloguing and speculating on the possibilities of what San Diego and Tijuana can do in relation to developing a supernatural urbanism, in particular the conditions along the border that are an extreme example of the two types of modernisations of the cities. The workshop also imparted to the students the ability to construct a vocabulary and the ability to become superheroes themselves. The InSite05 project was an attempt at incorporating those features into a new type of urban space. I would hope that we as designers and students emerging from an architectural education would develop a sensibility and reaction to the continual changes that are occurring with all of our cities.

04.
EMERG
EN
CE

ON THE EMERGENT LINE: COMPLEX SYSTEMS AND SELF-REGULATING ORDERS OF THE CITY

Rosalea Monacella

Introduction

The complexity of the urban periphery is difficult to capture through a singular line or figure on a map. The line, for instance, whether it is the border condition of the Mexico-USA border *la linea* or Mexico City's peripheral conditions, when captured is only a sign. The line is a sign for the political, social and environmental complexities that lie beyond the geographical orientating system of the map. For example, the dotted line on the map depicts a 'fence' between the US and Mexico yet ignores the complexities of control which are associated with this line. This line only marks out categorised limits according to jurisdictional authorities. This line does not express the activities of the Americans and Mexicans who patrol the border and the way they continually re-demarcate the line and redefine the territorial conditions of the two nations. Considering the legal or illegal transfer of goods, the transformations of the landscape through social interaction and natural causes the line is continual re-negotiated. In this sense the line does not necessarily demarcate an inside or outside, or where the US or Mexico begins and ends.

This chapter attempts to highlight ways in which landscape architects may treat the landscape and landscape representation. And through these new ways of treating landscape this chapter aims to produce new knowledge on border conditions, an issue especially relevant in the post-911 era where racial, religious and cultural classifications are increasingly becoming intertwined with geographical and architectural divisions.

To readdress some of these divisions this chapter will make use of morphologies that are not derived from rigid Cartesian geometries of measure and order. Here, I will look specifically at morphologies that are generated by responding to the continually differentiating and self-regulating landscape. Here, I will consider landscape form not as pure form that is detached from other pure forms but as a topological modulation which is interconnected with other topological modulations. As philosopher Manuel Delanda suggests, a topological form is 'a singular point in a manifold' capable of possessing 'different geometric properties' and 'physical forms' depending on the process of change and interaction it holds in a particular moment.[1]

1   Manuel Delanda, *Intensive Science and Virtual Philosophy*, New York: Continuum Books, 2002, 15.

By treating the landscape as a manifold in which forms are interconnected what is conventionally considered to be the line and the border condition change. Being aware of landscape forms being topological modulations the line that may be drawn becomes less a divisive mark and more a suggestive mark. The line is drawn not to demarcate permanent divisible territories but drawn to identify areas where ruptures once occurred and from which old territorial conditions may rupture again to bear new understanding and experience of space and ultimately citizenship and nationhood. The border becomes a line from which a field of possibilities may emerge.

Reconsidering what the term 'landscape' means can be used as an initial step into producing a line or lines that are also fields of emerging possibilities. These reconsiderations of the landscape may be carried over to a rethinking of the city, its borders, limits and potentialities. Within these reconsiderations of the landscape and the city I will suggest new ways to design for, to represent and to experience the contemporary city.

Landscape

The term landscape as used in this chapter and in the wider practice of landscape architecture is not meant to conjure up images of pastoral innocence hence designating an adjectival function. The term is also not intended to designate an object such as a piece of landed property. Landscape is neither a thing nor an adjective; it is a system of interconnected parts which relations are changing in time; as such the ways in which a landscape can be described remains indefinite. More importantly a landscape, insofar as the parts involved within it can themselves change in composition, and more or less parts can be added and subtracted, exceeds the limits of the self-contained object. In this sense a landscape cannot be reduced to the sum of its individual parts for the forces that constitute these parts and the quantity of parts involved are also changing. The order of the landscape so to speak is inherent in its process of transformation; in fact one may suggest that a landscape's 'order' may be a dynamic form of 'ordering' whence new groups of parts and forces are assembled or ordered and also whence groups of parts and forces are decomposed. In this section I will suggest that the landscape's re-ordering from a placid countryside to a dynamic field of change can be advanced by introducing changes to architectural drawing conventions.

The architect and theorist Greg Lynn succinctly describes this process of ordering and unity of parts, and most importantly the potential for emerging new spatial formation within a dynamic landscape:

> ...a landscape is a system where a point of change is distributed smoothly across a surface so that its influence cannot be localized at any discrete point...The slow undulations that are built into any landscape surface as hills and valleys do not mobilize space through action but instead through implied virtual motion...The landscape can initiate movements across itself without literally moving. The inflections of a landscape present a context of gradient slopes which are enfolded.[2]

2 Greg Lynn, *Animate Form*, New York: Princeton University Press, 1999, 29.

Following Lynn's description of a landscape one may say that its boundaries and form are given by its temporal dimension, otherwise its continual change. The new assemblages that are continually being forged in a landscape through social interactions and natural causes lay bare the forces that a landscape architect may harness in order to produce new assemblages of parts and forces to be interpolated back into the landscape.

In order to produce new assemblages that can be interpolated back into the landscape to change it, a landscape architect may begin by devising new ways to document or represent the landscape. These new representations of the landscape are meant to inspire the landscape architect him/herself and other interested parties to act differently, to inspire the future creations of designs that can also transform the landscape. Citing the art historian WJT Mitchell, landscape architect and theorist James Corner proposes a distinct between the mere picture and the image or what he considers the eidetic image. The picture depicts a city, a person or an object through the use of icons. The eidetic image on the other hand is able to affect its viewers to think. The eidetic image is the image that inspires the process of ideation.[3]

The eidetic image however must remain only suggestive, it must never take on the character of being didactic otherwise it will become the picture. The eidetic image is not the visual equivalent of any fixed concept. It may be composed of a set of graphic marks, texts and photographic images that together express the potentialities for new ideas to emerge; it offers to its viewers a number of forces and conditions to contemplate and to use to create new knowledge and experiences. In this sense the eidetic image cannot serve as the sole cause of the designs and ideas that follow. The eidetic image retains only an affective quality. Philosopher Gilles Deleuze writes that to be affected is not the same as being an effect of some sole cause. The cause and effect binary and the privileging of the cause do not figure in the process of being affected. To be affected, for Deleuze, is to undergo a process of modification in which form is a continual variation. As such to be affected implies the process where a subject, a concept or a space differentiates from itself.[4] Following Deleuze, Delanda writes that to be affected implies a certain degree of openness insofar as any individual or thing possesses an infinite quantity of capacities for change. Moreover, to be affected implies the capability to affect another individual or something else, hence to be affected is never a simple cause and corresponding effect equation but is constituted by a field of the actions of affecting and of being affected.[5] The eidetic image should be capable of inspiring this field of change.

In short one may suggest that the eidetic image should inspire the emergence of new becomings, to add new forces to current lines of becoming so that these current lines of becoming may move toward other kinds of becoming. The eidetic image differs from the mere picture precisely by refusing to turn the dynamic landscape into a series of separate programs and territories; rather it promotes the landscape's 'reality' which is its continual process of change. The eidetic image does not assume to be able to grasp the landscape's entirety, its multiple modalities and becomings. For a landscape architect the aim of making an eidetic image as Corner himself writes, 'is less to picture or represent these activities [such as the lines of becoming] than it is to facilitate, instigate, and diversify their effects in time.' Corner continues to suggest that making an eidetic image is 'a move away from ameliorative and scenographic *designs*', and move 'toward more productive, engendering *strategies*'.[6] The landscape architect designs strategies that affirm the landscape's infinite change in time; these strategies will activate the lines of becoming with immediacy. 'Eidetic images are fundamental stimuli to creativity and invention; they do not represent the reality of

3   James Corner, 'Eidetic operations and new landscapes', in James Corner (ed), *Recovering Landscape: Essays in Contemporary Landscape Architecture*, New York: Princeton University Press, 1999, 161.

4   Gilles Deleuze, *Spinoza: Practical Philosophy*, Robert Hurley (trans), San Francisco: City Lights Books, 1988, 48-49.

5   op cit, Delanda, 62

6   op cit, Corner, 159.

7   op cit, Corner, 163.

an idea but rather inaugurate its possibility.'[7] An eidetic image does not posit itself as posterior to or anterior to the changing landscape, it adds to it.

If eidetic images are stimuli to creativity and possibility then to encounter them may be said to be within what Delanda following Deleuze and Félix Guattari calls an 'intensive spatium'. For Delanda an intensive spatium is a space that is charged with intensity or more accurately a potentiality for change without these future changes being pre-planned. It is a space filled with individuals, objects and places that are ready to become something else. There is an utmost potentiality there; relations between individuals, objects and places as well as with ideas and concepts are

8   op cit, Delanda, 203-204.

primed for transformation.[8] When the viewer's ideas and concepts are encountered, his/her sense of subjectivity is not cancelled out by that of the eidetic image, rather, the forces of the eidetic image combine with those of the viewer to produce new ideas and concepts, subjectivity and spatiality. As Delanda notes, in the creation of 'heterogeneous assemblages' the components' differences are not cancelled by the process of homogenisation, instead becomings occur. Those new ideas and concepts, subjectivity and spatiality are precisely these new becomings taking place. Furthermore, the relations between these components or parts are 'non-decomposable distances',

9   ibid.

relations persists by changing.[9]

To facilitate the emergence of becomings and potentialities Corner draws attention to the ways the plan can be used to transform the conventional perspective of the landscape as essentially orderly as per the limits of Cartesian perspectivalism. Corner chose the plan mode of working because he believes that the eidetic images 'do not necessarily have to be radical and completely new; they may derive equally from a subtle realignment of the codes and conventions of some convention or

10 op cit, Corner, 164.

technique.'[10]

An eidetic mode of planning may proceed from a reworking of the architectural conventions of plan drawing. Corner cites the work of architects and theorists Rem Koolhaas and Bernard Tschumi among others to illustrate how architectural plan drawing conventions and imaginations of the landscape can be subverted,

> Rem Koolhaas, for instance, effectively altered traditional large-scale planning and diagramming from simply composing form and organizing program to completely *reformulating* form and program into freshly hybrid conditions. The dismantling and isolation of layers and elements in plan not only proposes a productive working method, akin to montage, but also focuses attention on the logic of making the landscape rather than on its appearance per se. Bernard Tschumi's work with notation and combinatory indexes further exemplifies the reworking or certain orthographic and

11 op cit, Corner, 164.

> choreographic conventions.[11]

For Corner 'the superimposition of multiple and sometimes incongruent layers in plan and section (evident in the works of both architects) has led to the generation of new possibilities'.[12] One may be able to form new spatial configurations and spatial understanding from juxtaposing a plan and a section onto one flat surface. The montage form is able to allow viewers to make new relations between two or more different architectural forms. In this sense one may say that the border or line that divides two or more architectural form is starting to fade; the two or more architecturals forms start to work together and becomes suggestive or a plethora of potential architectural forms that are yet to be determined in advance. Different architectural forms thus unite in the potential space they together may generate.

Corner also notes that statistics or pure data can be incorporated within the montage form to produce new relations. Here, he cites the work of contemporary urban designers such as design groups MVRDV and a-topos. These groups put together 'datascapes' which 'revisions of conventional analytical and quantitative maps and charts. Corner points out that these datascapes differ from conventional quantitative maps because they are designed to not only reveal the shaping forces of existing architectural, geographic, cultural and economical conditions of the city but also because they suggest ways to reframe these forces.[13] By revising these conventions the forces and processes operating across a given site can be revealed, and from these revelations new assemblages of forces may be constructed by other designers who may engage with these datascapes.

One can imagine the potentials at hand there can be if datascapes are combined with layered drawings that combine both section and plan views of varying scales. Such combinations are what Corner terms 'imagetexts'. Imagetexts are assemblages of texts, statistics, graphs, cognitive tracings, plans, orthographic projections and sections together with imagery that are 'unpicturable'; these are images proper to the process of thinking in which no image definable by proper Cartesian perspectivalism can be produced.[14] Indeed, texts used within imagetexts do not serve the conventional purpose of being labels, legends, keys, measurements or names. These texts may be snippets of poetry and theoretical musings which may not have direct or obvious relevance to graphs, plans and photographs on the same page. Readers of these imagetexts will have to forge possible relations between these texts and the graphs, plans and photographs juxtaposed next to them. These unpicturable images are images-in-process, fleets of forces being ordered into readable forms. These images are in the process of emerging; in fact emergence in time is their proper form. Corner summarises that:

> The landscape imagination is a power of consciousness that transcends visualisation…How one generates and effectuates ideas is bound into a cunning fluency with imaging. Similarly, the future of landscape as a culturally significant practice is dependent on the capacity of its inventors to image the world in new ways and to body forth those images in richly phenomenal and efficacious terms.[15]

12 ibid.

13 ibid, 165.

14 ibid, 166-167.

15 ibid, 167.

As Benjaminian scholar Susan Buck-Morss elaborating on the transformative qualities of the montage suggests, although the parts within a montage may be derived from the city, what these parts do and how they work together resist the harmonising perspective society conventionally ascribes to the city.[16] These parts in their new assemblage can be picked up by other designers and put toward new design productions. Ultimately, the montage format of the imagetexts and datascapes that Corner talks about are effective because they are eidetic, they inspire ideas to be produced, and these ideas can be plugged into other designerly activities that can physically, spatially, geographical and lastly architecturally transform the landscape, or more precisely add to the landscape's continual transformation.

16   Susan Buck-Morss, *The Dialectics of Seeing: Walter Benjamin and the Arcades Project*, Cambridge, MA & London: MIT Press, 1999, 225.

City

Classics scholar HDF Kitto writes that the ancient Greeks conceived of 'the polis as an active, formative thing'. For them the city was 'a living community' and not merely a collection of buildings and roads.[17] Following Kitto and the ancient Greeks' conception of the city one may suggest that the contemporary city with its active international trades, population migration and informational networks is in fact a dynamic landscape. Within the contemporary city there are extensive global forces that enable the emergence of spaces of continual movement. The contemporary city is no longer a place where the individual and the buildings are separate, or where buildings are merely effects or manifestations of fixed human subjectivity. The city, instead, is a site where the social being of a collective people is being produced. More importantly the identity of this collective people is continually changing due to the fact the constant interaction between individuals and between individual and objects will necessarily produce divergent voices, concepts and spaces. In this sense the collective people must also necessarily include the buildings, roads and other architectural forms, and vice versa; the built environment is inseparable from its biological companions. The city is an event comprised of interacting and self-differentiating parts.

17   H.D.F. Kitto, 'The polis: From the Greeks', in Richard Le Gates and Frederic Stout (eds), *The City Reader*, London: Routledge, 1996, 35.

Cultural theorists Michael Hardt and Antonio Negri suggest that the contemporary city possesses 'the power of the multitude', a term they borrow from medieval philosopher Benedict de Spinoza.[18] The multitude expresses a world filled with a multitude of forces in constant differential relations with each other. These forces can be grouped together to express subjectivities and spatialities that are themselves in the process of differentiation. Hardt and Negri elaborate:

18   Michael Hardt and Antonio Negri, *Empire*, Cambridge, MA & London: Harvard University Press, 2000, 47.

> The multitude is composed of innumerable internal differences that can never be reduced to a unity or a single identity – different cultures, races, ethnicities, genders, and sexual orientations; different forms of labour; different ways of living; different views of the world; and different desires. The multitude is a multiplicity of all these singular differences.[19]

19   Michael Hardt and Antonio Negri, *Multitude*, London: Penguin Books, 2004, xiv.

However, city as a multitude holds the risk of it being collapsed into nothingness or the postmodern capitalist celebration of pastiche which may imply the reifications and exploitation of cultures, peoples and spaces. Thus, for Hardt and Negri one must know how to harness this multitude of global forces so as to turn these forces against and deconstruct those stagnant or stultified assemblages that validate racial, economical and geographical divides.[20] One may suggest that the abovementioned cases of working against architectural drawing conventions as highlighted by Corner demonstrates a possible way of gathering up these global forces for the purpose of radical transformation.

20   op cit, Hardt and Negri, 2000, 47.

In order to be capable of working against conventions, as philosopher Paolo Virno suggests, one must:

> ...be accustomed to mobility, to be able to keep up with the most sudden conversions, to be able to adapt to various enterprises, to be flexible in switching from one set of rules to another, to have an aptitude for a kind of linguistic interaction as banalised as it is unilateral, to be familiar with managing among a limited amount of possible alternatives. Now, these requirements are not the fruit of industrial discipline; rather, they are the result of a socialisation that has its centre of gravity *outside of the workplace*.[21]

21   Paolo Virno, *A Grammar of the Multitude*, Isabella Bertoletti, James Cascaito and Andrea Casson (trans), New York: Semiotext(e), 2004, 84-85.

What Virno is advocating here is not to abandon work, which in our case is design. Rather, it is to rework the old conventions of design in order to forge new design methodologies and processes. One may pay attention to the unexpected outcomes within one's design process, work out how these outcomes are produced, what are the forces involved in their production and how these outcomes may be interpolated back into the city in order to change it, or at least create the conditions whence the potential for change can take place.

The 'political task' for artists, thinkers, writers and designers according to Hardt and Negri 'is not simply to resist these processes (taking place within old conventions) but to reorganize them and redirect them toward new ends'.[22] This is why when thinking of ways to transform stagnant and repressive border conditions it is never just a matter of retreating to the nostalgic homeland of one's forebears or claiming that borders do not need to exist at all. The process of radical design is not aimed at creating nothingness but aimed at a process of re-ordering existing conditions so that new subjectivities and spaces may emerge. In the case of the US-Mexico border it is not just making assumptions that the US is a major centre which is bullying its peripheral neighbours. It is not just a matter of celebrating Mexican culture as irrefutably 'local' whereas American culture is definitively global and oppressive. Hardt and Negri suggest that:

22   op cit, Hardt and Negri, 2000, xv.

> ...what needs to be addressed...is precisely the production of locality, that is, the social machines that create and recreate the identities and differences understood as the local. The differences of locality are neither pre-existing nor natural but rather effects of a regime of production.[23]

23   ibid, 46.

One needs to attend to the particular 'networks of flows' which produces a particular territory or local identity. One needs to attend to how these networks of flows of forces can be sped up again, dispersed and re-grouped otherwise.[24] The networks of flows of forces that constitute Mexican culture may partly consist of the global forces deriving from American culture by means of architectural and economical conditions such as US-owned factories in Mexican border towns. To attend to how Mexican culture may be liberated from these limiting conditions imposed by the factories is not to simply expel all American influences. Rather, it is a matter of knowing how to use these global forces so as to make them work to produce new kinds of subjectivities and spatialities that can transcend the now reified binary of American/Mexican. The post-colonial theorist Bill Ashcroft reminds us that the process of transformation is not necessarily contrary to the act of resistance. 'The most effective strategies of post-colonial resistance' he writes 'have not become bogged down in simple opposition or futile binarism, but have taken the dominant discourse and transformed it for purposes of self-empowerment.'[25]

The methodological-practical question we are concern with here is how will the forces that were once used to draw divisive lines between America and Mexico, American and Mexican, be put to different use so that the line becomes an emergent field. The US-Mexico border in this consideration is not obliterated, it remains, but how it is switched from a figure of division to a space for production marks its radicality as well as its ethicality. Deleuze reminds us that in a world criss-crossed with a plethora of values there can no longer be judgment based on higher moral values. Instead, Deleuze proposes that the modern individual functions upon a new kind of ethology based on the capacity to make new relations, subjectivity and spaces. This new ethology becomes:

> ...a question of knowing whether relations (and which ones) can compound directly to form a new, more 'extensive' relation, or whether capacities can compound directly to constitute a more 'intense' capacity or power. It is no longer a matter of utilisations or captures, but of socialibilities and communities. How do individuals enter into composition with one another in order to form a higher individual, ad infinitum?... Now we are concerned, not with a relation of point to counterpoint, nor with the selection of a world, but with a symphony of Nature, the composition of a world that is increasingly wide and intense.[26]

The promotion for the emergence of novel subjectivity and space is the radical political act, which creates a new kind of polis befitting of this new ethology for living.

If border towns in Mexico can be considered to be not the mere peripheries of the US-as-centre, then the reverse can also be considered: the United States of America and particularly its cities like Los Angeles and New York City are not impregnable centres, but also territories constituted and transformed by global forces. For example, a grid

24 ibid, 45.

25 Bill Ashcroft, On Post-Colonial Futures, London & New York: Continuum Books, 2001, 6

26 op cit, Deleuze, 1988, 126.

that frames and divides a city like NYC into rectilinear blocks does not necessarily indicate that the activities and programs within the city are as cleanly separated. Programs and activities can take place over several city blocks; more interestingly the area where these programs and activities may take place can have elastic boundaries. These boundaries can even be extended beyond the juridical borders of NYC given the fact as a global financial and cultural hub NYC is linked up to other global hubs via the internet, transport and flight routes, etc. Subsisting within NYC's grid is a field of emerging activities and programs that go beyond national boundaries.

When Hardt and Negri ask us to consider the production of locality of a place, we can infer that the question regarding the production of centrality is implied. We can ask what the social machines are contracting in global forces that constitute a centre or specifically an urban centre such a NYC or LA. Again, the methodological-practical question for landscape architects is how can existing conglomerates of global and also the more 'localised' forces be re-gathered? Architectural theorist Eduard Bru gives us examples of how the rigidity of a grid-ed city may be transformed. He gives Jean-Luc Goddard's films as an example. Goddard's films utilising 'techniques such as continuous changes of distance and viewpoint, fractured and elliptical dialogue' manage to transform Paris' arrondissement into 'a sort of periphery or outskirts'.[27] One may suggest here that Goddard's films by focusing on the minute events that occur on Paris' streets manages to express possibilities that the conventional overarching view of the city as a grid cannot express. Perhaps landscape architects can take a cue from Goddard's filmic techniques and begin to present cities from a ground-level, or perhaps, given today's advances in computer graphic technology, design diagrams that combine film, graphic design, programs, sound, plans, sections and orthographic projections so that amidst these juxtapositions a new understanding of space may emerge.

We can learn to respond to the complexities of time, scale and form within the city. We can become attuned to the complex self-regulating processes within the city such as the way paths are cut across playgrounds or how alleyways through alternative use become differently appreciated. We can pay attention to how different alleyways connect up with surrounding buildings and roads to form zones of radical appropriation. We do not merely trace what existed before but from observing these diverse activities we may learn to create new maps with new lines on them. Maps with multiple entrances and exits can be drawn.[28] Different kinds of media may be used to capture these processes of immanent change in the city. Such interdisciplinary ways of re-gathering the city's forces can open up the borders drawn within the city itself; it allows the city to connect with other territories and also to be connected with its unforeseen futures.

To speak of a city is to also speak of or suggest its potentialities for change, its potentiality for the racial, economical and cultural border within its juridical boundaries to be transformed. To speak of a city as landscape architects is to speak of how we can promote these transformations. The urban theorist Alex Wall writes that a

27   Eduard Bru, 'Objects and places', in Julian Raxworthy and Jessica Blood (eds), *Mesh: Landscape Infrastructure*, Melbourne: RMIT Press, 2005, 280.

28   Deleuze and Guattari write that 'contrary to tracing, which always return to the "same" a map has multiple entrances. A map is a matter of performance, whereas tracing always refers to an alleged competence (in reproduction), which reduces each desire and utterance back to a genetic axis or an overcoding structure, and which draws ad infinitum the monotonous tracings of stages on this axis or of constituents in this structure.' Gilles Deleuze and Félix Guattari, *On the Line*, John Johnston (trans), New York: Semiotext(e), 1983, 27.

29 Alex Wall, 'Programming the urban surface', in James Corner (ed), *Recovering Landscape: Essays in Contemporary Landscape Architecture*, New York: Princeton University Press, 1999, 233.

30 ibid.

31 ibid, 237.

32 ibid, 237.

33 ibid, 238.

city may be treated as an 'urban surface' which is 'dynamic and responsive; like a catalytic emulsion' capable of generating new urban, architectural and landscape forms comprising of new gatherings of forces.[29] The change that happens within a city is not telic; it does not necessarily need to move toward a utopian end forecast by jurisdictional and governmental authorities. The city's life does respond to the activities that its people perform. Again, as Wall reminds us, the city is a 'functioning matrix of connective tissue'[30] where an action performed or an alteration to the city's physical form can unfold a series of unexpected effects; a change in one assemblage of parts and forces can generate change in another and so forth. The life of a city, the macro and micro events that are taking place within it are not mapped out. The affective change between events will unfold in time; in fact, one may consider the city's surface to really be this event of unfolding.

Within this catalytic emulsion the border or line that demarcates function or specific program is replaced by a web of shifting relations, for in the dynamic city functions and programs themselves are also changing. Wall cites how the competition entry for the Parc de la Villete project by Koolhaas and the Office for Metropolitan Architecture (OMA) in the 1980s dealt with shifting programs. Parc de la Villette was a 121 acres piece of land that used to house an old nineteenth-century slaughterhouse complex. There were many logistical problems with it including site reclamation and modernisation of services. Additionally the client also asked for 'a bewildering and exhaustive list of programmatic demands'.[31] Instead of designing in terms of 'styling identity' Koolhaas and OMA for their competition entry were more concerned with designing design strategies that can 'accommodate any number of changing demands and programs'. Their response was to superimpose four strategic layers addressing different programs together in order to determine what new programs, functions and what new spaces corresponding to these new programs and functions may emerge. The four strategic layers are:

> The 'east-west strips' of varying synthetic and natural surfaces, the 'confetti grid' of large and small service points and kiosks, the various 'circulation paths,' and the 'large objects,' such as the linear and round forests.[32]

For Koolhaas and OMA the aim for producing this layered design was to offer the city 'a framework for developing flexible uses as needs and desires changed'. The drawings of the strips of synthetic and natural surfaces, service points and kiosks, circulation paths and those large objects were meant to slide over one another in order to allow for 'quantitative changes without loss of organizational structures'. Layering as a design technique allowed changes to take place without the need to cancel any programs. The sliding of these layers over one another meant that different programs may merge to form new programs that may result in new built forms.[33] This mode of designing allowed landscape architects to conceive of the city, or at least parts of the city, as a field of intermingling programs rather than a sectioned-up piece of real estate with each section being fitted with a given built form designated to accommodate only one program.

Temporal organisationS

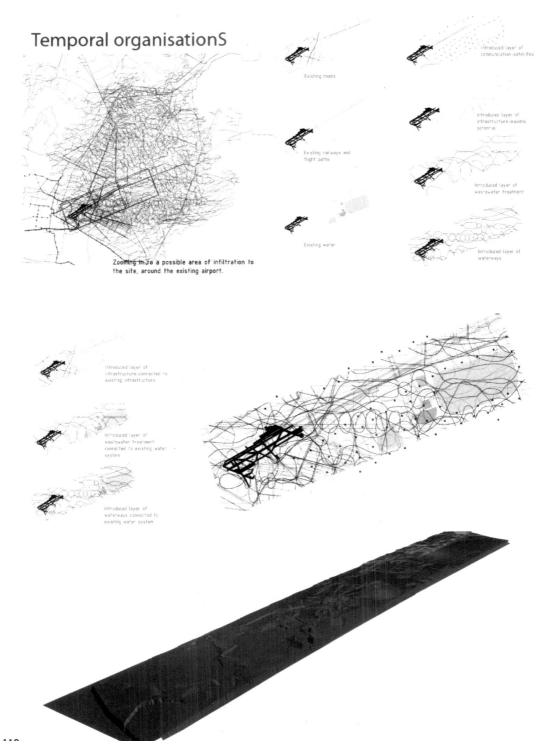

Zooming in to a possible area of infiltration to the site, around the existing airport.

Existing roads

Existing railways and flight paths

Existing water

Introduced layer of communication-satellites

Introduced layer of infrastructure-maximal potential

Introduced layer of wastewater treatment

Introduced layer of waterways

Introduced layer of infrastructure-connected to existing infrastructure

Introduced layer of wastewater treatment connected to existing water system

Introduced layer of waterways connected to existing water system

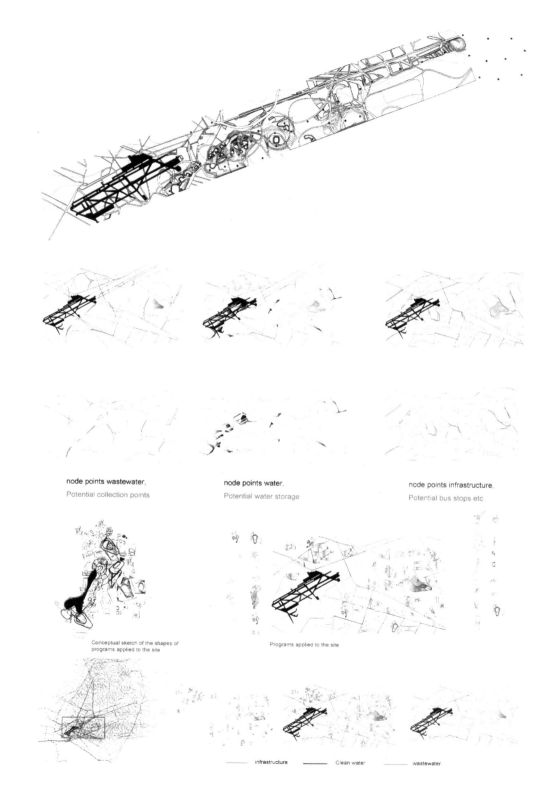

node points wastewater,

Potential collection points

node points water,

Potential water storage

node points infrastructure,

Potential bus stops etc

Conceptual sketch of the shapes of
programs applied to the site

Programs applied to the site

infrastructure _____ Clean water _____ wastewater

One can suggest that the layered drawings Koolhaas and OMA produced for their Parc de la Villette competition entry demonstrate the new kind of ethology that was mentioned earlier in this chapter. Their drawings do not determine what Parc de la Villette should look like. The drawings provided the graphic conditions for them (and one may suggest other designers) to think about the urban situation within that the piece of land that is Parc de la Villette – for instance, how different programs may integrate to form new programs – instead of simply ascribing to it a reified nineteenth-century Parisian stylistic identity. As Wall writes (and one can read this sense of new ethology into it):

> Thus, if the goal of designing the urban surface is to increase its capacity to support and diversify activities in time – even activities that cannot be determined in advance – then a primary design strategy is to extend its continuity while diversifying its range of services. This is less design as passive ameliorant and more as active accelerant, staging and setting up new conditions for uncertain futures.[34]

34   ibid, 233

Koolhaas and OMA's drawings express a certain eidetic-ness that Corner speaks about. These drawings prompt viewers to think of what can be made, not necessarily what must be built, but more so the radical design processes that may be developed to meet the challenges and nuances of the changing city.

Conclusions

The lines and borders that are drawn over maps in conventional cartographic practices are not completely useless to the landscape architect. The line cannot be completely eschewed. The landscape architect's task is to find out the forces contained on either side of these lines, and find out what forces constitute these lines, so as to regroup these forces into emergent fields from which new subjectivity and spatiality may spring. A line delimits nothing but still has a contour,[35] a contour which consequently influences the structure of future forms and consequently the dynamics of those forms. The line can be thought of not as a construction of definitive X,Y coordinates but a series of discrete sometimes imperceptible points where one point influences another causing a vibration to occur, shaking up old boundaries so that new territories may form.

35   Gilles Deleuze, *Francis Bacon: The Logic of Sensation*, Daniel W Smith (trans), London & New York: Continuum Books, 2003, 110.

The landscape architect's task is to evoke an operational dynamic of a landscape urban condition so that new ideas about the internal structures and differentiations within this particular landscape may take place. His/her designs become eidetic. To design is to affirm and sustain what architectural theorist Sanford Kwinter calls 'the epigenetic landscape', which affirms a landscape that bears tendencies or potentialities:

> The rivulets and modulations of the epigenetic landscape correspond to built in tendencies, or default scenarios, that would condition the evolution of forms in the hypothetical absence of supplementary forces acting over time. But one should not be fooled into taking the 'form' of the epigenetic

36 Sanford Kwinter, 'Landscapes of change: Boccioni's Stati d'animo as a general theory of models', in *Assemblage 19*, Cambridge, MA: MIT Press, 1992, 63.

landscape as itself 'essential', fixed, or predetermined. For it too is only a template or virtual form, assembled in another dimension, as a multiplicity generated by an extremely complex field of forces.[36]

A landscape architect draws lines that will open up to fields of emerging possibilities.

CONTRIBUTORS

Steve Biddulph

Steve Biddulph has been a psychologist specializing in parents and young children, for the last thirty years. His books are in four million homes worldwide, and published in 27 languages. For the last four years Steve has funded a range of efforts to improve Australia's treatment of boat people, especially vulnerable young families. With Beth Gibbings he co-directs the SIEVX Memorial Project, involving over 300 schools, churches and community groups.

Tim B Castillo

Architecture and Planning at the University of New Mexico. He is currently the Coordinator of Undergraduate Design and the director of the Laboratory for Digital Research. While at the University of New Mexico he has rigorously been pursuing new pedagogical courses that explore applications related to digital technologies. His studios and seminars continue to investigate new progressive strategies for design that are defined by informatics, digital media and CAD/CAM processes. In January 2007 Professor Castillo was recognized by the Association of Collegiate Schools of Architecture (ACSA) and the American Institute of Architecture Students (AIAS) as the National New Faculty Teacher for 2006-2007.

Tim B Castillo is the founder of Hybrid Environments, a critical design office that focuses on new technologies for architecture, research and design. His work has been published and exhibited nationally and internationally in various locations including the Institute for Advanced Architecture of Catalonia (Spain), Ecole Polytechnique Fédérale de Lausanne (Switzerland), Pavillon de l'Arsenal (France), Bienal of Sao Paulo (Brazil), University of Waterloo (Canada), University of Utah, University of Colorado, and the University of Texas-Arlington.

Tim received a Bachelor of Arts in Architecture from the University of New Mexico and a Master of Architecture from Columbia University. He has worked and consulted for many offices world wide including Skidmore, Owings and Merril in New York and Design Development International in Toronto.

Lawrence A Herzog

Lawrence A Herzog is Professor, Graduate Program in City Planning, School of Public Administration and Urban Studies, San Diego State University, San Diego, California. Herzog specializes in urban design and planning with an emphasis on Mexico, the Mexico-United States border and Latin America. Books include: Return to the Center: Culture, Public Space and City Building in A Global Era (University of Texas Press, 2006); From Aztec to High Tech: Architecture and Landscape Across the Mexico-United States Border (Johns Hopkins University Press, 1999); Where North Meets South: Cities, Space and Politics on the U.S.-Mexico Border (/University of Texas Press, 1990).

Herzog has served as Fulbright Scholar in Peru, and urban/regional planning consultant to the U.S. Agency for International Development (in Peru and Bolivia), the U.S. Embassy, Mexico City, the Environmental Protection Agency, and the American Institute of Architects.

Michael Kearney

Dr Michael Kearney is the RCUK Fellow in Law and Human Rights at the University of York. He received his PhD in International Human Rights Law from the Irish Centre for Human Rights at the National University of Ireland, and has worked as a legal researcher in the West Bank with Al-Haq, the Ramallah based NGO. His forthcoming book, The Prohibition of Propaganda for War in International Law, is published by Oxford University Press.

Troy Lovata

Troy Lovata earned a Doctorate in Anthropology, with a focus on the visual presentation of archaeological research, from The University of Texas. He was a Senior Lecturer in The University of Texas' Technology, Literacy and Culture Program and is now an Assistant Professor in the University Honors Program at The University of New Mexico, where he teaches courses and conducts research that focuses on public archaeology, the social role of technology, and the use of the past as cultural currency.

José Parral

José Parral studied landscape architecture at the University of California, Berkley and obtained an MA from the Architectural Association School of Architecture in London. Winner of the Rome Prize in Landscape Architecture 2006-2007. Visiting Professor at Ohio State School University Knowlton School of Architecture 2005-2006. He has worked for numerous landscape architecture firms such as Poirier Landscape Architects (San Diego, US), Pamela Burton & Company (Los Angeles, US), and Hood Designs (Oakland, US). The landscape projects that he has been involved in include: The Getty Center Central Garden (Los Angeles, US); Cummins Child Development Center (Columbus, US), and the North Campus Wedge, University of California, San Diego (San Diego, US). His work has been included in group exhibitions such as Otra/Another, Galería de Arte del Instituto de Cultura de Baja California (Tijuana, Mexico, 2003); The Machinic Landscape Exhibition, Universidad Nacional de la Plata (Buenos Aires, Argentina, 2002) and Projects Review, Architectural Association School of Architecture (London, UK, 2001). Parral currently lives and works in San Diego.

ACKNOWLEDGMENTS

STUDENTS
Laura Barrows
Hugh McCarthy
Kristie Howes
Paul Coffey
Jen Viol
Luke Maiden
Rob Barton
Shafee Jones-Wilson
Brett Milligan
Genieve Sanchez

LECTURERS
SueAnne Ware
Rosalea Monacella

Text by: SueAnne Ware + Rosalea Monacella
Images: taken during 2003 Borders workshop + study tour

SPECIAL THANKS
Armando Oliver Suinaga
Jose Parral
José Castillo
Dr Lawrence Herzog
IBERO University
San Diego State University
UDLAP
ESUA
Michael Howard
Craig Douglas
RMIT University (Landscape Architecture)
Cesar Torres
Tom Gooch
Cam Morris
Sean Hogan (Trampoline)